The Literacy Coach's Desk Reference

The Literacy Coach's Desk Reference

Processes and Perspectives for Effective Coaching

Cathy A. Toll

National Council of Teachers of English
1111 W. Kenyon Road, Urbana, Illinois 61801-1096

Staff Editor: Bonny Graham

Manuscript Editor: Amy Bauman

Interior Design: Doug Burnett

Cover Design: Pat Mayer

Cover Photo: Elizabeth Crews

NCTE Stock Number: 29684

Library of Congress Cataloging-in-Publication Data

Toll, Cathy A., 1956–
    The literacy coach's desk reference : processes and perspectives for effective coaching / Cathy A. Toll.
            p. cm.
    Includes bibliographical references.
    ISBN 0-8141-2968-4 (pbk)
    1. Reading teachers—In-service training—United States—Handbooks, manuals, etc.
I. Title.
LB2844.1.R4T65 2006
428.4071'5—dc22

                                                            2006004512

Contents

List of Figures and Tables

List of Black-Line Masters

Section 1: Introduction

This preliminary section of *The Literacy Coach's Desk Reference* provides an overview of the book, including its intended purpose, and some concepts about literacy coaching that will be useful as you read the rest of the book.

1 Purpose and Overview

Do you remember learning to ride a bicycle? You probably recall that it seemed impossible at first, and that the person helping you to learn gave you verbal directions such as, "If you start to fall, turn your front wheel in the direction of the fall." You may also recall that, mostly, the other person helped you by placing her hand on the back of your bicycle seat, providing steadiness and reassurance as she ran along beside you, ready to catch you if you fell. Learning to ride a bicycle is a complex task—one that can't be taught in a book but rather has to be tried by getting on a bike and pedaling, hopefully with someone there beside you.

Literacy coaching is similar to riding a bike in some ways. You learn to do it only by doing it. You can't become a successful literacy coach by reading a book. My current occupation is to serve as a consultant and teacher of literacy coaches, to be like the person who runs alongside the novice bicyclist. I refer to my work as coaching the coach. However, there is only one of me, and there is only a handful of others like me who work as full-time coaches of literacy coaches. Others—university professors, program coordinators, professional development consultants—spend part of their working lives supporting literacy coaches, but there still is not enough assistance. Literacy coaches are looking for more help, and this book is an attempt to provide that help.

Were I to write a book on how to ride a bike, one of the risks would be that I'd make bicycling too piecemeal, by providing a section on pedaling, a section on balancing, and so forth. Riding a bicycle is more holistic than that—once you have mastered it, it is nearly impossible to engage, either mentally or physically, in the separate parts involved in the rather complex act. I run the same risk in writing this book on literacy coaching. Coaching, which is much more complex than riding a bicycle, particularly because it involves working with people, is greater than its parts. Nonetheless, I believe this book will be of use to all of the literacy coaches seeking more assistance.

The phrase "literacy coaching" suggests action, yet most of the literature on the topic is about the content of literacy coaching rather than the process. To compare this approach to coaching with another activity, you could say this would be comparable to writing a book on cooking and telling only about categories of food and varieties of cooking utensils, not about how to chop, dice, simmer, and perform all the other tasks necessary for cooking. It is helpful for cooks to know about utensils and food groups, just as it is helpful for literacy coaches to know about literacy instruction and literacy learning. However, one will never become successful as a cook or a as literacy coach with only such knowledge. One must also understand and practice the processes involved.

The comparison between literacy coaching and cooking is apt, too, because one can cook a simple meal with only a little learning but may spend a lifetime refining one's skills as a cook. So, too, a literacy coach might have success with only a little skill and knowledge but could spend a lifetime refining those capacities. An even better comparison might be to driving a car or even performing surgery. It would be impossible—and dangerous—to try to learn such complex tasks in a book, and the author of such a book would no doubt oversimplify these tasks in order to make the book clear. So it is with literacy coaching: I've written a book about it that provides instructions on various processes, but in order to make the processes clear, I've oversimplified them a bit. What I've written about each process is accurate and useful but, when put into action, will be more complex than when described in writing.

This is not a "recipe" book. When I cook, I typically find a recipe that looks interesting, access all the ingredients, and follow the steps to prepare the food. I end up with a passable meal, but nothing more. I tell friends that I can follow recipes, but I'm not a "cook" in the sense that a cook understands how to take ingredients, add herbs and spices, and maximize their potential by preparing them in the most suitable fashion. Such cooking requires more knowledge and skill than I have, but, more than that, it requires decision-making abilities that I lack. I follow recipes; I don't cook.

Literacy coaches who open this book and follow it step-by-step will, in a similar fashion, be able to adequately perform the duties of their job, but they won't be able to "cook" in the sense that they are active decision makers. They won't be taking the ingredients of their situation—teachers, working with students, facing particular challenges or possessing particular interests, in the context of a specific school in a specific community—and working with them as creative decision makers.

So what good is this book? A great deal of good, I hope, as a starting point, as a reminder, and as a reference. This book provides the basic ideas; literacy coaches, as they immerse themselves in their experiences, provide the "spice." I shaped the title, *The Literacy Coach's Desk Reference*, after the title of a book that medical doctors use, *The Physician's Desk Reference*. Physicians use their desk reference book to quickly seek information about pharmaceuticals, including effects, side effects, contraindications, and dosing recommendations. In other words, *The Physician's Desk Reference* is an essential resource to help medical doctors make decisions. I hope *The Literacy Coach's Desk Reference* can do the same by helping literacy coaches to make decisions about their work.

Please use this book to remind yourself of important processes to use when coaching. Use it as a review before going into a new or challenging situation or as an opportunity to fine-tune your practices as you reflect upon them. Use it as a decision-making tool, not a recipe book. In other words, use the information, suggestions, and strategies in this book to enrich your perspective as you decide what to do while coaching, not as step-by-step instructions that you must follow to a "T."

Organization of This Book

This book is organized to maximize its usefulness for literacy coaches. This first section provides essential background information about the book but more importantly about literacy coaching. Please read this section first in order to contextualize my understanding of literacy coaching and to provide further perspective on literacy coaching as you read and use the ideas in the rest of the book. In particular, Chapter 2 of this section provides an overview of the different purposes of literacy coaching, the roles literacy coaches might play, and the outcomes of various approaches to literacy coaching. I hope this chapter frames the choices made when a literacy coaching program is developed and implemented, choices that significantly affect the nature and effect of the program. I hope, too, that Chapter 2 enables you to understand the perspective that influences my choices in creating processes for literacy coaching.

The next sections of the book focus on the formats in which literacy coaching most commonly takes place: conferencing with individual teachers, meeting with small groups, providing demonstration lessons, providing services to the entire school, and providing services to individual students. These sections, and the chapters within them, can be read in any order as needed; each stands independently from the others. On the other hand, occasional references in any particular section will build upon other sections, most notably some of the material in the first chapter of Section 3, which provides ideas for using processes in small group meetings that are similar to those used in individual conferences. Although readers can understand all chapters and sections without referring to other chapters or sections, they may want to refer to related material in other parts of the book as well. The book concludes with a chapter that summarizes significant points in the book and makes general suggestions for the field of literacy coaching.

Each chapter, except for the two in this introductory section and the concluding chapter, follows the same format:

Overview: The first page of the chapter provides a brief description of the topic, its purpose, and how it can be implemented, along with questions to think about before, during, and after that process. Black-line masters found later in the chapter are summarized on this page as well. Because users of this book may open it to any chapter, according to their needs, the overview page is provided to help readers "warm up" to the topic at hand. In addition, this page engages the reader with a general approach to coaching practices and perspectives that would be easily evident to someone reading the entire book from front to back but might be missed or forgotten by readers who turn to any individual chapter by itself.

Discussion: The topic is then discussed in greater depth, to provide background information, helpful tips, rationales for the processes, and any other suggestions that may be useful.

Sample Coaching Session: Chapters will include vignettes providing sample coaching sessions. These vignettes are attempts to bring the ideas in that chapter to life. They are not provided as "scripts" for literacy coaches to memorize and replicate. Literacy coaches tell me repeatedly that it helps them to see and hear what effective literacy coaching is like, and these vignettes will provide an opportunity to do that, albeit in the reader's imagination. Some of the vignettes, especially those in the earlier chapters, are rather brief and end abruptly, in order to focus readers' attention on the key point discussed in the chapter. As subsequent chapters present more complex aspects of literacy coaching, the vignettes become longer and more complex. A few chapters in the later sections discuss literacy coaching tasks that cannot be represented easily in vignettes and therefore no vignettes are included.

Black-Line Masters: Most chapters will conclude with one or more black-line masters that are provided for easy copying and use. These forms and reference sheets are offered as suggestions, any one of which will be useful to some literacy coaches and not needed by others. A few topics don't lend themselves to black-line masters, and, therefore, there will be none in those chapters.

I believe readers will find the format of the chapters useful for several reasons. First, it provides an overview to "set the mood" and help the reader prepare for the discussion of the topic. Then a more complex detailed description of the topic is provided, along with an example. These components should help readers learn and review important literacy coaching processes. In addition, placement of black-line masters within each chapter will make them easily accessible. Finally, the familiar pattern of each chapter will make it easy to refer back to any part of the chapter on any topic.

How I Come to This Work

I found my way to literacy coaching by accident, in the sense that I did not set out to be a literacy coach, much less a coach of coaches. However, looking back, I can see with clarity how I ended up at this point. My teaching experience provided a broad perspective: I taught students in elementary school, middle school, high school, and university levels. My leadership experience strengthened many skills: I served as a reading specialist, curriculum coordinator, school principal, director of research and development, and grant director. My scholarly work furthered my theoretical and research background: I investigated teacher professional development, school reform, theories of power and change, and literacy leadership. And my experiences as a consultant gave me practical tools for making a difference: I worked with teachers and administrators in schools, districts, and regions all over the United States, including rural, small town, urban, and suburban communities.

The overarching goal of my career has been to help schools make sense for the kids and adults who spend their days in them. I served in numerous capacities that had coaching-like duties, including work I did as a teacher leader, reading specialist, principal, and consultant, and more recently, I have served as a coach of coaches. This coaching work always made sense to me, and therefore I hoped it made sense to others, because it started with the concerns of teachers, administrators, and literacy coaches. In addition, it was embedded in "real" work in schools and had the flexibility to take place with individuals or groups of educators. Finally, it brought out the best in all involved: I was able to use my best skills of relationship-building, planning, and knowledge sharing while helping others to use their best skills in observing, assessing, problem solving, and reflecting. Literacy coaching at its best is teaching and learning at their best.

I believe that there is a myth about educators that holds that good teachers have no problems. This myth influences teachers early in their careers, usually when they are still in their undergraduate preparation and thinking about student teaching. Preservice teachers *know* they will have problems when they begin teaching, and therefore they are frightened. Later, in their own classrooms, many practicing teachers attempt to hide their problems by closing their classroom doors and rarely talking about teaching in any but the most superficial ways. What these preservice and inservice teachers fail to recognize is that experienced teachers have a lot of problems. In fact, I'd suggest that teaching is *about* problem finding and problem solving. It is the mark of good teachers to struggle but also to admit that struggle, turn to resources for help, and develop a reflective habit of mind that enables them to use all data (broadly defined to include a range of information at hand about students and students' learning) in developing practices and trying to solve problems.

You can probably see why literacy coaching makes sense to me. Literacy coaches are superbly positioned to support teachers as problem solvers. For those teachers unfamiliar with or uncomfortable with conceptualizing themselves as people who have problems and work to solve them, literacy coaches provide gentle support in discovering this reality. For those teachers comfortable with problem finding and problem solving, literacy coaches are trusted colleagues who share parts of the journey, traveling alongside teachers as they do the difficult and rewarding work of wrestling with the dilemmas that will always arise. Moreover, literacy coaches support teachers in developing strengths necessary not only for addressing any current problem but also for preventing future problems and therefore achieving more success. Coaches do this when they work alongside teachers to pursue topics of interest.

All of this talk about problems may leave readers thinking that my approach to literacy coaching coincides with the current trend of teacher bashing. It is hard to open a newspaper today without finding some supposed evidence of the failure, laziness, or lack of caring of teachers. This latest round of attacks upon teachers began in 1983 with the Reagan administration's publication of *A Nation at Risk* (National Commission on Excellence in Education, 1983) and has ebbed and flowed in the years since, particularly as certain politically-driven movements have captured the attention of the media and the public. Thus, as additional well-publicized reports have been issued, as presidential initiatives have been promoted, and as selective research has received attention, teachers have been blamed for myriad faults. In this vein, literacy coaching might seem like the "cure" for ineffective teaching, and some educators and policymakers do see coaching that way.

For me, though, literacy coaching is not about broken teachers but about teacher strengths. I describe the work of literacy coaches as "helping teachers to identify their strengths, 'grow' those strengths, and develop new strengths" (Toll, 2005, p. 5). This focus on strengths is not a Pollyanna-like optimism, blinded by reality. Rather, it reflects my twenty-five-plus years working with teachers and defining myself through it all as, first, a teacher. I know that every teacher has strengths and every teacher is successful in some ways. Moreover, I know that the trend in teacher bashing is politically motivated and reflects the use of certain "lenses" that enable the viewer to see teaching in a preordained way. For instance, there are those who use their particular perspectives to see schools as bastions of iniquity because they attempt to provide an education to all students, no matter the students' apparently innate capacities. These individuals would rather that schools spend a good deal of time and money on the more "gifted" students and less on those with less "potential" (Shannon, 1998). My use of quotation marks probably cues you in to the fact that I disagree with this perspective. However, it is found in certain circles, not least those groups who would like school vouchers to enable some parents to send their children to some publicly-paid-for schools that deny admittance to apparently less-capable students (Spring, 1997).

Given that each perspective on schools and teaching has a political component (yes, even mine), each perspective on literacy coaching has a political component as well. I feel some concern that this book reflects a rather limited view of teaching and coaching. For instance, the educator and theorist Alan Luke (1995) has illustrated that the emphasis placed on strategies-and-skills-for-understanding in most reading instruction today, which he places in categories of coding competence and semantic competence, encompasses only about one-quarter to one-half of the possible literacy work that could be done in schools. I wish that the schools in which literacy coaches worked exemplified this insight by going beyond that limited scope to what Luke refers to as pragmatic and critical competences, but they rarely do. Therefore, the examples of literacy instruction that I provide in this book are drawn from instruction that focuses mainly on strategies and skills for understanding. I want this book to resonate with readers and to provide examples that seem "real" to them; as a result of my interest in writing about "what is," though, I fail to write about "what could be" in literacy instruction.

In addition, the processes of literacy coaching described and exemplified herein imply that there are logical steps to get from point A to point B and that these steps are always the same. But literacy coaching, like any other complex work, isn't that simple. However, I rely primarily on language to address literacy coaching practices and perspectives, and language that is sequential and explicit seems the best way to write this book. Perhaps a better author could write poems or draw sketches to explain the complex, rich, and sometimes intuitive aspects of literacy coaching, but I lack those skills. I trust that readers of this book are smart enough to know that breaking processes into steps is a good way to describe them, but that few processes are as simple as those descriptions.

To provide further insight into possible ways in which literacy coaching could be thought about and written about, in Chapter 2 I'll provide an overview of various models of literacy coaching and the perspectives they reflect. In this way, readers will be able to better understand various approaches to literacy coaching and will see why I make many of the choices that I do as a literacy coach and coach of coaches.

2 Roles and Formats for Literacy Coaching

Distinctions among literacy coaching models, programs, and practices can be made when answering three questions: (1) Coaching for what? (2) What do literacy coaches do? (3) What will be the outcome? I will discuss these three questions in order to help readers understand important distinctions among approaches to literacy coaching and to elucidate the decisions I've made in developing the processes that make up the bulk of this book.

Coaching for What?

Establishing the purpose for an activity is important to ensuring that one accomplishes what one set out to do. However, the question of why literacy coaches coach is not always asked. Literacy coaching has swept into existence so quickly that many literacy coaches find themselves in their positions without ever thinking about what they are coaching *for*. I see three purposes for literacy coaching: teacher remediation, program implementation, and teacher growth.

Teacher Remediation

As discussed in the previous chapter, the myth of the ineffective teacher is alive and well in the twenty-first century (Bracey, 2004). In response to the perception that teachers are unable to do their jobs, some educators advocate for coaching to fix the problem of teachers who are doing a poor job. For instance, the Learning First Alliance, a coalition of twelve national educational organizations, describes the failure of teachers in *Every Child Reading: A Professional Development Guide:*

> The new understandings of how children learn to read, why some fail, and how best to teach have yet to be applied on a widespread, consistent basis. Teachers may be educated, licensed, and employed without knowledge of the most important tools for fighting illiteracy. (2000, p. 1)

The report's authors later advocate coaching as an essential part of the solution to the problems they describe:

> New teaching skills must be practiced and refined with support and coaching. Coaching—which may be provided by peers, con-

tent experts, or supervisors—is an important aspect of professional development. (p. 9)

In describing such a purpose for literacy coaching, I use the word *remediation* to emphasize the underlying assumption that teachers have been diagnosed as in need of repair. Most advocates of literacy coaching for this purpose use terms such as "scaling up student achievement" or "increasing teacher effectiveness." However, one thing is clear: coaching is sometimes conceived as corrective action to address inadequacies among teachers (see, for example, Carelli, 2004).

Program Implementation

Literacy coaches are sometimes expected to coach for program implementation. This is especially evident in some Reading First programs (Central Regional Reading First Technical Assistance Center, 2005) and in the America's Choice program (National Center on Education and the Economy, 2002). In both instances, a program of instruction is spelled out, including the use of particular assessments and instructional materials, and teachers are expected to follow the program exactly. To ensure that they do this, literacy coaches are hired to monitor program implementation, model correct implementation, and assist teachers in fine-tuning their efforts.

Teacher Growth

Literacy coaches are sometimes hired to promote and support the growth of teachers. Those who hire literacy coaches for the previous two purposes—to coach for improvement and for program implementation—would argue that they, too, wish to promote teacher growth, and they are accurate. However, the target in coaching for teacher improvement is teachers who are flawed or broken, and the target in coaching for program implementation is teachers who must accurately implement the specifics of a particular program. The target in coaching for growth is teachers who have goals and interests and benefit from support in reaching them. In other words, the growth is self-directed.

I'd suggest that efforts to help a teacher change that are not self-directed are generally not really about growth, in the positive sense of the term, and are instead about forcing teachers—whether gently, urgently, or in a manipulative manner—to fulfill someone else's vision of teaching and learning. So, for instance, if a school principal tells a teacher that she must work with a literacy coach in order to develop more effective ways to help students comprehend, the coaching serves the purpose of remediating the teacher's limitations. On the other hand, if a teacher determines that she wants to be more effective at helping students comprehend, the coaching serves the purpose of growth. To an extent, this is an arbitrary distinction among words, but it is not an arbitrary distinction among concepts. Coaching because someone has told a teacher to change is very different from coaching because a teacher wants to change, and I'm using the terms *improvement* and *growth* to represent the two concepts.

As you might guess, these three purposes for literacy coaching are not entirely compatible. For instance, if a coaching program is targeted at program implementation, the direction for teacher growth is already set. Sometimes teachers are excited about such implementation and, because they see the goals of the program as consistent with their own goals, they are being coached for growth as well as program implementation. Sometimes, though, these goals don't coincide.

I would like the term *literacy coaching* to be used only to describe work that supports teacher growth. I recognize that teachers have flaws like all human beings and for some individuals those flaws are so great that remediation may be an appropriate approach, but I see that task as one led by a supervisor, not a coach. This work may be necessary, but it damages the field of coaching if it is labeled as such: teachers become self-conscious that because they are working with a literacy coach, they have been identified as in need of repair.

On the other hand, some schools and districts have chosen to use a program or plan that must be implemented in a very specific way. This can be true of initiatives as different as Reading Recovery and the Dynamic Indicators of Basic Early Literacy Skills (DIBELS) reading assessment. In such a case, the term *implementer* rather than *coach* would be more effective. When one is identified as an implementer, it is clear that there is one task to do: implement the program or plan. On the other hand, if one is called a coach for this kind of task, it seems as though there is more to the task than that. Using the label *coach* for a program implementer confuses those who wish to coach primarily for teacher growth.

I choose to emphasize teacher growth as the purpose of literacy coaching because it seems both professionally and morally sound. I agree with educators who claim that teaching involves extensive reflection and decision making (Clift, Houston, & Pugach, 1990; Zeichner & Liston, 1996), and coaching for teacher growth supports this vision. Moreover, the view of teachers developing and working toward their own goals is consistent with my vision of teaching and learning as multilayered and complex, not something that can be spelled out by a program and not something that can be "cured" from outside the context and experience of teaching itself. In addition, coaching for a purpose that supports teachers in meeting their goals seems "right" in the sense that it honors the worth and dignity of teachers. This is consistent with my value system. Some readers may think, "Yes, that's well and good, but what about those teachers who *aren't* doing their jobs?" Again, this is a supervisory matter, not a coaching matter, and should be addressed as such.

What Do Literacy Coaches Do?

Although at any moment any particular literacy coach might be performing a variety of tasks, there are four categories of tasks that literacy coaches perform: modeling expertise, monitoring, serving, and collaborating.

Coaches Model Expertise

Some literacy coaches model certain approaches to instruction, classroom organization, or assessment. In doing so, they show others a practice that is considered effective, preferable, or even best, as in the term *best practices*. These terms form a continuum, referring to practices that may be among those that are chosen ("effective") to practices that are considered *the* practices to use ("best"). Borrowing from the educational thinker Frank Smith (personal communication, 2005), I use the term *demonstration* to signify the former and *model* to signify the latter.

Coaches Monitor

Some literacy coaches monitor teachers. This monitoring may be for the purpose of improvement or program implementation, but in either case it places the coach in a quasi-supervisory position. When coaches monitor, they judge, to determine whether teachers have adequately improved or accurately implemented, thus engaging in tasks typically performed by supervisors.

Coaches Serve

Some literacy coaches speak of "servicing" teachers, a term that may be borrowed from special education teachers who provide "service" to students and classes. Coaches who are serving teachers seem to be subservient to teachers. In other words, in these situations coaches and teachers aren't collaborators. Rather, coaches wait for teachers to take the lead by approaching them, telling them what they need, and receiving the coaches' service in filling those needs. Many literacy coaches who have formerly served as reading specialists may be in the habit of using this wait-and-respond approach, perhaps because their time to work with teachers was limited, given the other duties they performed. However, the clients of literacy coaches are teachers, and literacy coaches must take the initiative to work with all teachers in the potential pool of colleagues. Moreover, although "serving" conveys a comfortable notion of being of help, it also implies a passivity that may not lead to effective literacy coaching. I encourage literacy coaches to be collaborators in their work with teachers.

Coaches Collaborate

Literacy coaches collaborate when they partner with teachers to support teachers' growth. Collaboration is about using the strengths of all involved. There may be a facilitator or a leader, but there is no one participant whose ideas or words are more important than any others'. When collaborating, teachers and literacy coaches listen and learn from one another, reflect together, and strengthen their relationship through the process. In fact, in collaboration, the relationship is as important as the outcome. If collaborators achieve a productive, mutually-respectful relationship, they will have the capacity for ongoing work together that will garner benefits over time, regardless of any particular outcome. Collaboration is difficult but worthwhile (DiPardo, 1997; Supovitz, 2002). In fact, a good deal of this book is about how to make collaboration effective.

What Is the Outcome?

The greatest difference among particular programs of literacy coaching appears to be that they aim for different results. Some results are more superficial than others, and some results seem to last longer. I stress to literacy coaches the importance of thinking about the outcomes desired by their work and the assumptions about teaching and teacher learning that are inherent in each possible outcome.

Changing Teacher Behaviors

A great deal of literacy coaching leads to behavioral changes. Like all professional development that focuses only on behavioral change (Loucks-Horsley, Love, Stiles, Mundry, & Hewson, 2003), literacy coaching aimed at changing behaviors rarely has a lasting effect. When changes involve only behavior (or "practices" in the parlance of many coaching programs), teachers lack insight into why they are changing and how to adapt for new challenges that crop up in the teaching environment. For instance, if a teacher is taught that posting word walls is an important behavior and therefore puts a word wall on her bulletin board but doesn't know why she is doing it, she is unlikely to make the word wall effective for her students. Or if a teacher is taught to post a word wall and engage in "making words" (Cunningham & Hall, 2005) but doesn't have an understanding of how graphophonic systems work in language (Goodman, Watson, & Burke, 1993), she may not provide students with making-words activities that help them to be more effective readers.

Supporting Teachers' Comfort with Changes

Literacy coaches recognize that teachers generally work hard and want to do what's best, and, as a result, some literacy coaches decide that the best outcome of their work is to support teachers as they do their work. When coaches aim at teacher comfort as the outcome they desire, they emphasize being friendly with teachers, finding resources to help teachers with their work, and seeking other ways to "help out." The literature on professional development doesn't address teacher comfort often, although the Concerns-Based Adoption Model (C-BAM) is a well-respected exception (Hord, Rutherford, Hurling-Austin, & Hall, 1987). The C-BAM model is a useful tool for literacy coaches wishing to gauge teachers' responses to innovations and then to respond appropriately to those teachers.

Developing Teachers' Habit of Mind

The outcome of some literacy coaching is that teachers routinely identify problems, reflect, collect a broad array of data, kid watch, and solve problems. In other words, such teachers develop habits of mind that influence the way they think about their work and students' learning. When this occurs, teachers understand the reasons for the decisions they make and the actions they take, because they have thought about them themselves rather than being told to do them by someone else. Of course, many teachers already possess such habits of mind, and for them literacy coaching focused on this outcome will reinforce and support their ongoing work.

Developing Teachers' Habits of Interaction

Sometimes literacy coaching supports the development of collaboration and inquiry among groups of teachers on a school staff or in a district. In these cases, teachers develop reflective, problem-solving habits of mind as they work with their colleagues, but they also develop habits of interaction. Teachers engaged in collaborative coaching projects work in an atmosphere of respect and relationship building, where the strengths of all involved are shared and considered. When such teams of teachers conduct inquiry, they advance their capacities to explore "big" questions and to collect and analyze a great deal of data in order to answer those questions. In the best of all collaborative situations, participants create methods and attitudes that enable difference to thrive in the group. In other words, such teams find ways to work together even when they don't agree and to grow and learn even when they have complex data that don't point to single answers.

Putting It Together

Figure 2.1 summarizes the ideas I have just presented. It shows each of the three ways I've conceptualized coaching: based upon what coaches are coaching for, the tasks coaches perform, and the outcomes that are sought. Models of coaching are often developed according to one of these approaches to conceptualizing the field. Each is informative, and I would encourage literacy coaches and others to consider all three factors. However, I believe that looking at outcomes is a wise approach when considering deciding how to implement literacy coaching. After all, models are representations of theories, and the categories of outcomes better reflect theories of change and teacher professional development. In addition, looking at outcomes is consistent with the school of philosophical pragmatism that notes that the value of any statement, action, or plan can be gauged by how well it produces the results desired. Finally, looking at the outcome sought is a useful way to distinguish among various programs of literacy coaching that are in existence, whereas the other two categories are less useful in making distinctions among programs.

Certainly, programs of literacy coaching will include multiple purposes, roles, and desired outcomes. Coaching is complex and occurs in the complexity of schools. However, I find it is helpful to think about where one's priorities lie in these areas and to understand the possible choices that might be made. In this way, literacy coaches and other educators can be precise in their understandings of literacy coaching and can spot contradictions in the ways they have conceptualized coaching.

The ideas about literacy coaching outlined in this chapter support the approach to coaching reflected in the rest of this book. The processes emphasized in this book prompt teachers to be reflective decision makers. Some chapters describe processes that lead to habits of teaming as well. All processes described here promote the role of the literacy coach

Purposes for Coaching
Teacher remediation
Program implementation
Teacher growth

Coaching Roles
Model
Monitor
Serve
Collaborate

Coaching Outcomes
Change teacher behavior
Change teacher comfort and attitude
Change teacher habits of mind
Change teacher interaction

Figure 2.1. Purposes for coaching, coaching roles, and coaching outcomes.

as a collaborator. I strive to provide processes that reflect my answers to the questions: What are the purposes of literacy coaching? What does the literacy coach do? What are the outcomes?

Section 2: Processes for Individual Conferences

This section focuses on processes used by literacy coaches to conference with individual teachers. There is a sequence to some of the processes—for instance, arranging conferences naturally occurs before the actual conferences take place—but there is also a recursiveness to them. For example, upon starting to plan for action, a teacher and literacy coach may realize that they want to revisit the problem in order to clarify the outcome and goal. Therefore, I encourage readers to look through this entire section and then use the processes in any convenient sequence. In addition, I hope readers recognize that these processes often flow into each other. I take them apart here in this section for the ease of discussing various aspects of the coaching conversation, but in reality they are not often clearly distinguishable from one another.

3 Arranging Individual Conferences

Overview

What

- Arrange individual conferences in advance.

Why

- To ensure a convenient time for the teacher.

How

- Approach the teacher, with a calendar in hand.

To Think about in Advance

- How will I explain my request for a conference?

To Think about During

- How hard should I persist if the teacher refuses a conference?

Black-Line Masters Included in This Section

- **Individual Conference Scheduling Form.** This form can be used to track your meetings with teachers. List all teachers in the pool of teachers with whom you might meet on the left side. As you schedule a meeting with a teacher, write the date of that meeting in the first blank space to the right of the teacher's name. Put a single line through that date when the meeting has occurred.
- **Individual Conference Reminder Note.** This note can be used to remind teachers of an upcoming meeting with the coach. Merely fill in the spaces and drop it in the teacher's mailbox the day before a meeting. Don't forget to sign your name at the bottom of the note.

Discussion

Some literacy coaches wait for teachers to come to them asking for help, or they invite teachers to sign up for meetings with the coach. These approaches are not always successful because not all teachers respond. I encourage coaches instead to arrange meetings with all those teachers within the "pool" of teachers to be coached. In other words, if the literacy coach's job is designed to provide support to all teachers in a middle school, then that coach would arrange to meet with all of the teachers in that school, either alone or in teams, at the coach's initiative. In another school, if a literacy coach's job description indicates she or he will work with the teachers in grades K–3, then the coach would arrange meetings with all teachers in that group.

Savvy coaches ask their principals to explain the expectations of literacy coaching at the start of the school year or at the start of the coaching program. The principal might emphasize her or his expectation that all teachers (or all teachers in a specified group) collaborate with the coach and stress the desired outcome of building teacher capacity. The coach might then mention the process she or he will use to schedule conversations with teachers in order to start the process.

Always schedule a meeting with a teacher rather than dropping in on that teacher on the spur of the moment or catching the teacher in the hallway or lunchroom. In this way, you and the teacher will be sure to set aside time for your conversation and nothing else. Usually, an individual conference requires at least thirty minutes. When possible, meet with the teacher in her or his classroom, which will no doubt be the most comfortable for the teacher. Meeting in the teacher's classroom also makes it easier for the teacher to show you schedules, student work, or other materials that may enhance the discussion.

Think ahead of time about how you will explain your interest in meeting with the teacher. I encourage literacy coaches to develop an introductory statement about the purpose for meeting that:

- Does not single out any particular teacher or group of teachers (e.g., "As you know, I'm asking to meet with all of the teachers in the building.")

- Does not indicate that there is anything wrong with the teacher (e.g., "My purpose is to listen and learn about what you are doing in your classroom and how your students are doing.")

- Indicates your interest in supporting the teacher (e.g., "In this way, perhaps we can find ways that I can support you in helping your students achieve more.")

- Indicates your expectations about time (e.g., "I hope we might find thirty minutes to talk.")

If the teacher expresses hesitation or lack of interest, persist to a reasonable extent in establishing your interest in meeting with the teacher. The chart in Table 3.1 provides some ideas for how to do so.

The challenge to persisting is knowing when to continue to ask for a meeting and when to let it go. Literacy coaches need to "read" teachers' body language and tone of voice and trust their intuition about how much to persist. I advise that it is better to let the issue go and return in a couple of weeks than push hard and lose teachers' interest entirely. Keep in mind that your objective is to start a conversation—not to create an enemy or manipulate a colleague.

Table 3.1. Responding When Teachers Hesitate to Make an Appointment

The Teacher Says:	You Say:
Thanks, but I don't have any time at all to meet with you.	I hear you. Could I check back with you in two weeks to see if your schedule has opened up a bit?
I don't have my calendar handy.	When is a good time for me to check back with you, when you will have your calendar nearby?
I just don't need any help from you.	That's OK. We don't have to talk about help that you need. I'd like to listen and learn about what you are doing and how I might support you—not because you need my help but because I am here to support all the teachers in the building.
I won't give up my free time to meet with you.	I understand. Could I make a trade with you? If you will give me thirty minutes of your planning time, I'll read to your class for thirty minutes, so you can make up that time.
Everything is fine in my classroom. I am succeeding just the way things are.	Great. Could we still talk, so I can listen and learn? It helps me to know about the strengths of the staff, so I can support those strengths and also so I can learn from them. Also, I'd like to be able to share your successes with others who may be looking for ideas or for a classroom to visit.

Sample Coaching Session: Scheduling 1:1 Conferences

Coach (walking into classroom just after the children have been dismissed for the day): Hi, Mary. Do you have a second?

Mary: Sure. What's up?

Coach: As you know, I'm scheduling appointments with each of the teachers in the school. My hope is that we can meet for thirty minutes so I can listen and learn about what you are up to and how I can support you in helping your students to be successful.

Mary: Well, OK. But you know everything is really going well in my classroom, and I just finished my master's degree in reading. I don't think there's anything new you can teach me.

Coach: I'm glad to hear things are going so well. And congratulations on your degree. I'm glad to hear you are up-to-date, because my role isn't really to teach you, it is to support you.

Mary: How would you do that?

Coach: That's what we can talk about when we meet. Could you spare a half hour?

Mary: Well, I suppose, but I'm really busy right now with this new math program.

Coach: OK, what if we waited a couple of weeks? Do you have any time during the week of the twenty-first?

Mary: Only before school.

Coach: That works for me. Could we meet at 7:30 on Tuesday the twenty-second?

Mary: All right.

Coach: Great. I've got it on my calendar, and I'll send you a reminder just before then.

INDIVIDUAL CONFERENCE SCHEDULING FORM

Teachers' Names	Meeting Date	Meeting Date	Meeting Date	Meeting Date	Meeting Date	Meeting Date	Meeting Date	Meeting Date
1.								
2.								
3.								
4.								
5.								
6.								
7.								
8.								
9.								
10.								
11.								
12.								
13.								
14.								
15.								

INDIVIDUAL CONFERENCE REMINDER NOTE

Hello,

This is a reminder that we have a conference scheduled for the date and time listed below. I look forward to this opportunity to listen and learn about what is going on in your classroom and to seek ways in which I can support you in your efforts to help students achieve.

See you then!

Teacher's Name:

Date and Time of Conference:

---

4 Getting Started

Overview

What

- Begin conferences in a friendly yet productive manner.

Why

- A conference should feel like a conversation, but one that has a purpose.

How

- Chat casually and then review the purpose of the conference.

To Think about in Advance

- Am I approaching this meeting with an open, neutral mind, free of preconceptions about the teacher or about how the conference will go?
- If I have met previously with this teacher, what did we talk about last time?

To Think about After

- Did I create a relaxed yet purposeful start to our conference?

Discussion

It may seem simple: One has a conversation by, well, conversing. What's to think about or prepare for? On the other hand, we all know intuitively that starting a conversation with the right tone can optimize the chance that it will be a success. This is as true when convincing a spouse or partner to buy a new car as it is when creating a comfortable atmosphere for a coaching conference.

Conversations typically begin with small talk—that is, with talk about things that are relatively unimportant and irrelevant to the main part of the conversation. This will probably happen in a coaching conference as well, which makes sense if you want the conference to feel like a conversation. However, if the conference is to become a *professional* conversation, it needs to move beyond small talk to talk about teaching and learning. Occasionally, the teacher may guide this transition, but often, especially in a teacher's first few coaching conferences, this role is left to the literacy coach.

An effective way to make the transition from small talk to professional conversation is to review the purpose of the conversation. If this is your first meeting with a teacher, you will again say something similar to what you said when you set up the appointment. You want to remind the teacher that

- You are there to listen and learn.

- You want to think about how you might support the teacher in doing what she or he is already trying to do—in other words, coaching will add to the teacher's strengths and efforts, not repair them.

If this is not your first coaching conversation with a teacher, then an effective way to begin is to review what you and the teacher talked about in your previous meeting and the goal you set at that time for the current meeting. Your aim is to provide a brief summary for both you and the teacher, in order to help you both recall the previously agreed-upon purpose for meeting again.

Transitioning into the "official business" of the conference with a teacher is quite simple. On the other hand, if a literacy coach is not prepared and centered, that transition may not take place, or it may take place in a confusing manner. In either case, such a transition will not provide the smooth and productive start to a conference that you are wishing for.

Sample Conversation: Getting Started

Teacher: Come on in. I'm just cleaning up after a science lesson— what a mess!

Coach: It looks like the kids really had a hands-on experience here.

Teacher: Yeah, we were weighing water and sand, and then we got carried away and started weighing other things we found in class. The kids were really engaged, and they asked great questions, but it was messy.

Coach: Here. Let me bring the trash can over there.

(Teacher and coach finish the clean up.)

Teacher: OK, sorry about that. Now I can focus on our conversation.

Coach: Great. I brought my notes from our last meeting, where we talked about your guided reading groups and your concern that you need to change the make up of the groups more often. We discussed some ways to do that, and you were going to try regrouping the kids before we met again. We decided that at our next meeting, we'd talk about how that regrouping went. . . .

5 Focusing

Overview

What

- Direct attention—yours and the teacher's—to the teacher's concerns.

Why

- You begin to listen and learn—the essential step in effective literacy coaching.

How

- First meeting: Ask the teacher to tell about anything interfering with her or his goals.
- Subsequent meetings: Ask how it's going.

To Think about in Advance

- Am I prepared to ask a question that will encourage the teacher to continue the conversation?

To Think about After

- Did the conversation flow smoothly from my "starting out" review to the teacher providing information about how it is going?

Black-Line Masters Included in This Chapter

- **The Question.** This master provides The Question for starting out in several forms. Literacy coaches are encouraged to attach one or more versions of The Question to their clipboards in order to assist them in remembering the phrasing of this important tool.

Discussion

Focusing is really the second part of starting out. The first part, discussed in the previous chapter, is transitioning from small talk to a productive professional conversation by summarizing the reason for the meeting. Focusing, then, takes place when the literacy coach moves the conversation from a one-sided *talking to* the teacher to an interactive conversation, begun with a well-phrased question.

- Questions that can be answered with yes/no.
  - Is there anything I can do to assist you?
  - Do you have a goal with which I can help you?
- Questions that establish a dependency relationship between coach and teacher.
  - Can I help you meet your goals?
  - Would you mind if I showed you a different way?
- Questions that indicate inadequacy on the teacher's part.
  - How can I help you improve?
  - What are you doing to change your instructional practices?
- Questions which provide too much direction.
  - How are your guided reading lessons going?
  - Could I demonstrate shared writing in your classroom?

Figure 5.1: Unproductive focusing questions.

If the meeting is the first one between the literacy coach and the teacher, the literacy coach wants to ask a question that continues a conversation. In most cases, the teacher will be eager to talk with the coach, but in some cases the teacher may not be as interested. Some questions asked at this point could be used by the teacher to shut the conversation down. Examples of such unproductive questions are in Figure 5.1.

The questions in Figure 5.1 are unproductive because they could be answered with a single word—"No"—or with a negative phrase, such as "You can't." Savvy literacy coaches instead will ask a question that demonstrates recognition of teachers' strengths and yet allows teachers to tell something about a struggle or challenge that they are encountering. I have developed such a question, one that I recommend, because it almost always results in a productive conversation. Here it is:

> When you think about the reading and writing you want your students to do, the teaching you want to do, and the classroom you want to have, what gets in the way?

This question assumes that teachers do indeed have a vision for their work and that they are indeed striving to make that vision a reality, but that things get in the way. It is effective, I believe, because these are assumptions held by most teachers as well. Thus, the question recognizes teachers' desire to succeed and to help their students succeed but also acknowledges that there are obstacles to this work.

Literacy coaches can use variations of this question for varying situations. For instance, with a content-area teacher, a coach might ask:

> When you think about the understanding you want your students to have when they read and write about [insert content discipline here, such as geography or physics], what gets in the way?

Sometimes literacy coaches are asked to focus on a particular aspect of literacy instruction or a literacy program, such as guided reading or teaching vocabulary. I'd encourage program leaders to reflect carefully about whether such an approach is best in promoting teacher growth, because it may assume that all teachers are focusing on the same particular aspect of their instruction or program and it may also place undo emphasis on program implementation—that is, behaviors and practices—rather than reflection and decision making. However, I recognize that coaches sometimes have to comply with such a requirement. In these instances, a variation on The Question above might take this form:

> When you think about the way you want to implement [guided reading, vocabulary instruction, etc.] and when you think about the kind of reading and writing you want students to do as a result, what gets in the way?

A fourth "shape" to The Question reflects the emphasis some districts place upon using data for decision making. It goes like this:

> When you think about the data you have about student reading and writing and when you think about helping your students strengthen their reading and writing, what gets in the way?

I caution coaches to be especially careful when using this variation of The Question, for several reasons. First, many teaches believe that the word *data* refers only to test score data. Of course, it doesn't; *data* could refer to any information that teachers have collected, including information that results from classroom observations, in-process reading assessments, miscue analyses, interviews, conversations with parents, assignments, and many other sources. However, unless teachers and literacy coaches all think about *data* in a broader manner, this version of The Question may be too limited. In addition, teachers sometimes interpret a question such as this to imply that teachers don't understand their students—only data do. Again, this isn't necessarily the case, and most literacy coaches recognize that teachers possess a great deal of information—or data, broadly defined—about their students. But unless teachers understand the intent of the use of the term, literacy coaches may want to be cautious when speaking of data. I often simply substitute "information," and then teachers are much more comfortable. On the other hand, administrators sometimes want to know that coaches are discussing data with teachers, so I include the question in the format above.

These questions are printed on a master sheet later in this chapter. You may want to make a copy of that page and attach it to a clipboard that you carry with you when conferencing with teachers.

If you have met previously with a teacher and wish to focus a subsequent coaching conversation, the nature of the focusing question should be a bit different. You already have an ongoing conversation with that teacher, so you are not attempting to start one. Rather, you want to regenerate the conversation in this subsequent meeting and, if you started out with a review of the previous meeting, all it usually takes is an open-ended question. I use, "How's it going?" as my focusing question because it provides some room for the teacher to choose the direction of the conversation. While first reviewing the previously agreed-upon purpose for the conference, the literacy coach and teacher are "tuning in" to the conversation and to literacy-related topics. Then, by asking "How's it going?" the coach is giving the teacher control over the direction the conversation will take. Rarely at this point do teachers digress to a nonprofessional topic. Rather, teachers either pursue a further aspect of what was talked about last time, such as their effort to try a new idea or learn new information about the topic that was discussed, or they raise a new issue that is even more important than the previous topic.

For instance, a teacher who worked with a literacy coach to develop new ways to help students read a science textbook might respond to "How's it going?" with a discussion of a new strategy that helped her students. On the other hand, if a new student who speaks little English joined that teacher's class in the previous few days, the teacher may indicate that she would rather talk about how to help that student than continue the discussion of textbook-reading strategies.

Occasionally a teacher will raise a new topic at every coaching meeting. If this occurs, the literacy coach may want to ask for the teacher's help in focusing the conversation on one topic at a time. Another strategy that the coach might use is to be candid but neutral in observing that the topics have changed each week. The coach could ask the teacher for insight into why that is the case or for help in staying on one topic for a bit, in order to be more focused.

Moving the coaching conversation from the starting point to a productive professional interaction is relatively easy, but literacy coaches are wise to think ahead about how they will guide that transition. Without preparation, a conversation may stall in the opening stages and feel aimless or like a waste of time.

Sample Coaching Session: Focusing

> *Coach:* Thanks for meeting with me. As you know, I'm meeting
> with all of the teachers to listen and learn about what they are

up to and to see if there are ways I can support you as you help your students succeed.

Teacher: Uh-huh.

Coach: So I guess I'd like to start by asking, when you think about the kind of learning you want seventh-graders to do, the kind of understanding you want them to get from reading and writing social studies materials, and the kind of teaching you want to do, what gets in the way?

Teacher: Well, everything would go really smoothly if the kids would just do their homework. But they won't. I've tried rewarding them, testing them, punishing them, calling their parents—but I just can't get the kids to do the reading assignments at home.

Coach: Can you tell me some more about that?

Teacher: Well, I try to cover a chapter every two weeks. There is a lot of material in each chapter, so I have a lot of teaching to do. Plus, I want the kids to have discussions in class and to have time for work that isn't related to the textbook. In order to get that all in, the kids have to do something at home. I figure reading the book is the best thing for them to do outside of class.

Coach: Mmm hmm.

Teacher: But they won't do it!

Coach: I hear a lot of frustration in your voice. It sounds like you've tried a lot of tactics to get the kids to read.

Teacher: Like I said, I've tried positive and negative consequences. They just don't want to do it.

Coach: What happens when the kids try to read the textbook?

Teacher: Well, they hate it. It's, well, it's a textbook, it's not MTV or a video game—you know, they have to pay attention and work to understand it.

Coach: Hmm.

Teacher: These kids just don't want to do anything that requires them to work.

Coach: So I hear that it is work for the kids to get through the textbook.

Teacher: Yes, but they're seventh-graders. They can handle it.

Coach: Do *any* of the kids do the reading?

Teacher: Well, yes, the stronger students, the ones who do their other homework, do my assignments, too. But the rest . . . they just make up excuses.

Coach: What would you like to do?

Teacher: Throw out the textbook! *(laughs)*

Coach: (chuckling) Maybe that's not such a bad idea. Is the book absolutely necessary?

Teacher: Well, I have to reteach all the important points anyhow. But it does seem that the kids should be reading and doing their homework. It's the principle of the thing!

Coach: I hear you. This isn't how we imagined it would be when we were preparing to be teachers and thought about the students we'd have someday, is it?

Teacher: Right.

Coach: But you say you've tried just about everything. It seems to me there are two choices: find some approach to getting the students to do their homework that you *haven't* tried yet or find an alternative to the reading homework.

Teacher: Hmm. When you put it that way . . . I guess you are right.

Coach: Does one of those options appeal more than the other?

Teacher: Well, I can't think of any other way to get the kids to read the textbook, so I'm afraid I'm left with the alternative.

Coach: It seems that an alternative could take many forms—an alternate reading assignment, an alternate assignment, an alternate way to read the textbook (but not at home), no assignment—there are several options. I'd be glad to help you think about those options and decide what you'd like to do. Would you care to work with me on this?

Teacher: Well, sure. I guess so. . . .

THE QUESTION
(with variations)

When you think about the reading and writing you want your students to do, the kind of teaching you want to do, and the kind of classroom you want to have, what gets in the way?

When you think about the understanding you want your students to have when they read and write about [insert content discipline here, such as geography or physics], what gets in the way?

When you think about the way you want to implement [guided reading, vocabulary instruction, etc.] and when you think about the kind of reading and writing you want students to do as a result, what gets in the way?

When you think about the data you have about student reading and writing and when you think about helping your students strengthen their reading and writing, what gets in the way?

6 Gathering Information through Questioning

Overview

What

- Gather information that leads to setting goals.

Why

- A coach's priority is to listen and learn when a teacher presents a problem or interest.

How

- Ask questions that will lead the teacher to describe the situation in detail.

To Think about During

- Do I have a good understanding of what the teacher is describing? How do I know that my understanding is accurate?

To Think about After

- Which questions were effective in encouraging the teacher to tell me more?

Black-Line Masters Included in This Chapter

- **Questions for Gathering Information.** The master provided in this chapter is designed for use by literacy coaches in facilitating coaching conferences. It may serve as a review for coaches or as a "cheat sheet" that could be placed nearby during a conversation and referred to as needed. On the other hand, it may be a tool you want to place on your bulletin board and review occasionally for new ideas.

Discussion

The first job of a literacy coach is to listen and learn. I'm repeating this statement several times in this book, because it is so important and so easy to forget. Individuals who choose to be literacy coaches often do so because they want to make a difference; in other words, they want to help make things better. Because of this urge, literacy coaches are often quick to come up with solutions to problems and challenges—often too quick.

When coaches provide solutions before taking time to listen and learn, they risk several problems. They may give the impression that they are the experts and the teachers aren't. This is always a danger because we all know some things, and it is disrespectful and sometimes alienating to approach teachers as if coaches were the only knowledgeable ones. In addition, coaches who quickly provide solutions may steer the conversation in a direction that it doesn't need to go. For instance, a literacy coach might hear a teacher express concern about students' ability to write persuasive essays and begin providing solutions about helping students develop their arguments using graphic organizers, when really the teacher's concern is about helping students understand their audience. Although the two issues are related, the conversation could go for some time before the teacher's concern is revealed. A third danger in failing to listen and learn is that it assumes that the coach's role is to "fix" teachers' problems, when it isn't necessarily that at all. Remember, a coach first wants to support teachers' strengths and help teachers develop new ones. Sometimes, the best way to do that is to listen and learn and to ask good questions in the process.

Good questioning is the key to gathering information. I encourage literacy coaches to develop a repertoire of questions that encourage teachers to tell more and therefore enable coaches to listen and learn. A convenient way to think about such questions is to divide them into five categories:

- Questions to open up a conversation
- Questions to learn more about a particular problem or situation
- Questions to explore solutions
- Questions to plan for action
- Questions to forward the action

I'll provide more information about using these questions as part of the goal-setting, action-planning, and forwarding-the-action processes in the next three chapters. Here, I'd like to focus specifically on the questions.

Figure 6.1 highlights characteristics of effective questions for gathering information. Each of these characteristics increases the chance that a question will prompt a teacher to feel comfortable in telling more and that a coach will learn more.

- Are open-ended: Questions require more than a one-word response.

- Are devoid of judgment

- Contain carefully-chosen words: A bland word is better than a spicy one (*problem* rather than *crisis*; *disorganization* rather than *mess*; *struggling* rather than *failing*).

- Are asked in a neutral tone of voice with body language signifying openness (comfortable eye contact, shoulders turned toward teacher, arms uncrossed)

- Use "I" more than "you" if discussing a negative response ("I'm confused" rather than "You aren't making sense.")

Figure 6.1. Characteristics of effective questions.

Opening Up a Conversation

A coaching conversation can only take place if there is a conversation. In other words, both the coach and the teacher need to be talking. However, early in the process of gathering information, the teacher typically does most of the talking. Therefore, coaches' questions at this point are short and very open-ended. The question I find most useful at this point is, "Would you say some more about that, please?" Often I use a statement rather than a question: "Say some more about that." Without fail, this request leads to a greater opening up on the teacher's part, and I learn a great deal more.

Another coaching strategy at this point is to check one's understanding. To do so, a literacy coach tells what she or he has heard. The coach might say:

> Let me make sure I understand the situation. Your students are eager to read and read rapidly with few miscues. However, it seems they don't understand what they are reading. Did I get that right?

A third effective strategy is mirroring. "Mirroring" is a practice used by psychologists and others when they want to help another person notice what they are experiencing. To do so, one acts like a mirror for the other, by stating what one observes or hears. This is similar to the strategy described above, making sure one understood correctly, except that it has a different purpose. When mirroring, one is less concerned with one's own need to make sure one has heard correctly and more concerned with helping others know they have been heard. In the process, the others sometimes learn more about their own thoughts and feelings or at least bring more self-knowledge to their conscious awareness. Here is how mirroring might sound:

Teacher: I give up. I've tried everything to get my students interested in reading—special times, rewards, showing them my own love of reading—and nothing works. These kids just don't want to read.

Coach: Wow, I hear the frustration in your voice. You really want the kids to love reading, don't you?

A caution in attempting to mirror: Don't repeat verbatim what the other person has said. Some of us have heard that repeating exactly what was said demonstrates active listening. However, when a person is frustrated, such repetition can be annoying or even seem to minimize the person's concerns, because the literacy coach seems to be responding in a rote fashion rather than responding as a sincere, listening colleague. For more on mirroring, check the information from Mark A. Sircus at http://www.worldpsychology.net/World%20Psychology/VirtualPsyFiles/ayahuasc22.htm.

Learning More about a Problem or Situation

Questions to learn more about a problem or situation should move the conversation toward specifics. Early in the conversation, a teacher may speak generally about a frustration. As the conversation moves along, the literacy coach can help the teacher describe the situation in greater detail, which will enable both parties to understand it better and to gather information that may help in considering possible solutions.

I find a few question stems are useful at this stage of the conversation:

- What does it look like when . . . ?
- What does it sound like when . . . ?
- What are the students doing when . . . ?
- What have you tried to . . . ?

Questions with these stems provide an opportunity for both teachers and literacy coaches to reflect upon the situation at hand and to gather detailed information about it. Responses to such questions help literacy coaches to get closer to "seeing" and "hearing" the problem or dilemma as well as helping them to better understand how teachers have attempted to address the matter.

Questions to Explore Solutions

When the coach has listened and the teacher has described the situation at length, it is time to consider solutions. Before I move into the "solution" phase of a coaching conversation, however, I check with the teacher to see if that is what she or he prefers. I do this both out of courtesy (I do it for my friends as well) and to make sure that the teacher is seeking a solution. Occasionally, we want to vent our frustrations without needing to solve a problem. Typically, once a teacher has worked with a coach, the teacher realizes that literacy coaching is oriented toward helping teachers grow their strengths by finding and solving problems or identifying and meeting goals. However, teachers, like all humans, still occasionally need to let off steam.

To make sure the teacher wants to move into problem-solving mode, I ask something like, "I hear that you want to find ways to help students write more successfully in biology class. I'd be happy to help you with that. Would you like to explore some alternatives?"

Preparatory work in problem solving takes place in a coaching conversation when the teacher has described a problem or situation and the coach has listened and learned. This problem identification provides a foundation upon which the coach and teacher can identify a goal, develop a plan of action, and forward the action. Identifying a goal is really the process of finding a solution to a problem. At the point in the coaching conversation where such a goal is set, neither participant knows whether the problem will indeed be solved by meeting the goal because the goal has yet to be put into action. Therefore, a goal is a best guess of what might solve a problem or address a challenging situation.

Questions that assist teachers in developing best-guess solutions—i.e. in framing goals—are those that optimize the chances that the guess is correct. In other words, the coach's questions invite teachers to "try on" a goal and see if it fits. Just as a wise shoe buyer considers a pair of shoes by trying them on and asking questions ("Are they comfortable?" "Is it easy to walk in them?" "Do they make my feet look attractive?"), so coaches and teachers want to inquire into a possible goal.

I find these questions to be especially helpful in gathering information about a possible goal:

- What will your classroom be like if you do that?
- How will your students be different if you meet this goal?
- What will it look like in practice? Sound like?
- Does this goal seem consistent with your beliefs about students/ literacy/learning?

These questions can be used in the goal-setting process described in Chapter 7.

Questions to Plan for Action

After a suitable goal is developed, the coaching conversation focuses upon planning for action. In order to try the solution represented by the goal, the teacher needs to do something differently. The step of planning for action seems to appeal more to those who think sequentially by nature. Those who view the world in more holistic terms may feel frustrated at the idea of planning for action—they just want to take action! However, even the most holistic among us benefit from thinking about what it will take to implement a goal. This line of thinking may come more naturally or comfortably to some than others, but it will be of value to all.

The questions asked by a coach to gather information at this point will be focused on action steps, a timeline, resources (human and material), and a method for evaluating the plan when it is implemented. For each aspect of the plan, there are one or two key questions.

Steps

What is the first thing you want to do to meet this goal?

What will you do next?

Timeline

When would you like to start?

Can you imagine a point where you will consider the plan to be fully implemented? When would that be?

Resources

Is there anyone else you want to turn to for help in meeting the goal?

What materials do you need?

Evaluating the Plan

What will it look like/sound like if the plan is successfully implemented?

What information will you need to gather in order to decide if the plan is successful?

How will you know if the plan is successful; what criteria will you use?

Questions such as these will help literacy coaches and teachers create a plan for putting a goal to the test. These questions will help to create a vision for teachers' work and will give the coach valuable information to use in forwarding the action.

Forwarding the Action

The concept of forwarding the action will be discussed in detail in Chapter 9. Here, I want to provide questions for gathering information about forwarding the action. What readers need to know at this point is that "forwarding the action" describes steps coaches and teachers take to make sure that the plan for action does become action. In other words, forwarding the action ensures that ideas developed in the coaching conversation become reality.

Questions that help coaches at this step in the process include:

- How's it going?
- What's getting in the way?
- What have you tried so far?
- What else could you do?
- How can I help?

Once again, these are open-ended questions, designed to prompt teachers' thinking, not to do the thinking for teachers. By using questions such as these, coaches support teachers as professionals and avoid co-opting teachers' ability to think for themselves.

The questions for gathering information in this chapter are designed to facilitate coaching conversations and to make the processes described in other chapters of this book more successful. These questions will help literacy coaches to do their first job, which is listening and learning, at all stages of coaching.

Sample Coaching Session: Gathering Information

Teacher: I'm so frustrated with Sean—he's a new student in my class. He won't read anything!

Coach: Tell me more, please.

Teacher: Well, during reading workshop, Sean just sits there. When I ask him why, he shrugs his shoulders.

Coach: Have you had any opportunity to listen to him reading?

Teacher: Yes, I've done two running records with him, and I've looked at the miscues in both. He seems to be constructing meaning, and his miscues for the most part are productive.

Coach: Hmm, he sounds like a mystery.

Teacher: I don't believe kids are naturally lazy, but I'm starting to worry that that's true of Sean!

Coach: What else do you know about Sean?

Teacher: His family just moved here from St. Louis. He has a sister in kindergarten. I met his parents on Sean's first day of class, and they seemed interested in school and in wanting to communicate with me.

Coach: What would it be like if this problem were solved?

Teacher: When it was time for independent reading, Sean would read.

Coach: Does anything need to change any other time?

Teacher: Well, actually, no. Sean seems to participate all the other times, and he is attentive when I read aloud to the class.

Coach: So we're only talking about independent reading. Do I have that right?

Teacher: Yes. Hmm . . . that's an interesting observation. I wonder what it is about independent reading.

Coach: What are some possibilities?

Teacher: Well, he may need more help in selecting books, although I've had two conferences with him about that, so I don't think so. He might be unable to pay attention during independent reading—there are some buddy readers in class, and I'm doing Guided Reading groups during that time, so there is a lot going on. He might be unable to sustain his attention for some reason. Or maybe he doesn't like to read. Oh, and I wonder if he knows what independent reading is for and how to do the journaling and reading logs correctly.

Coach: You've got quite a few ideas there. I've jotted them down as you've talked—do I have all of them?

Teacher: Let's see . . . mmm . . . uhm mmm, yes. You got them all!

Coach: How would you like to proceed?

Teacher: Well, I need to get more information to see if any of these hunches are right. I think I'd like to develop a plan for observing Sean and also using the Burke Reading Inventory with him.

Coach: How can I help?

Teacher: Well, here's an idea . . .

QUESTIONS FOR GATHERING INFORMATION

To Open Up the Conversation:
- Could you tell me more . . . ?
- Can you say some more about that, please?
- Here's what I think you are saying. . . . Is that accurate?
- May I read my notes to you to see if I understand what you are saying?

To Learn More about a Problem or Situation:
- What does it look like when . . . ?
- What does it sound like when . . . ?
- What are the students doing when . . . ?
- What have you tried to . . . ?

To Explore Solutions:
- What will your classroom be like if you do that?
- How will your students be different if you meet this goal?
- What will it look like in practice? Sound like?
- Does this goal seem consistent with your beliefs about students/literacy/learning?

To Plan for Action:
- What is the first thing you want to do to meet this goal?
- What will you do next?
- When would you like to start?
- Can you imagine a point where you will consider the plan to be fully implemented? When would that be?
- Is there anyone else you want to turn to for help in meeting the goal?
- What materials do you need?
- What will it look like/sound like if the plan is successfully implemented?
- What information will you need to gather in order to decide if the plan is successful?
- How will you know if the plan is successful? What criteria will you use?

To Forward the Action:
- How's it going?
- What's getting in the way?
- What have you tried so far?
- What else could you do?
- How can I help?

The Literacy Coach's Desk Reference: Processes and Perspectives for Effective Coaching by Cathy A. Toll © 2006 National Council of Teachers of English.

7 Setting Goals

Overview

What

- Assist teachers in stating goals for solving problems or addressing situations.

Why

- A clear goal statement is useful in planning for action and forwarding the action.

How

- Listen and learn as each teacher describes the situation or problem and then invite efforts to make a goal statement.

To Think about in Advance

- Is the teacher ready to begin thinking about a goal?

To Think about During

- From where is this goal coming?
- Do the teacher and I have enough information about the problem or situation in order to develop a goal?
- Is this goal realistic?

To Think about After

- Is the goal stated in a way that is meaningful for the teacher?
- Do the teacher and I have a clear sense of what the situation will be like if the goal is met?

Black-Line Masters Included in This Section:

- **Individual Conference Record Sheet.** Use this form to take notes on the entire conference and copy it for the teacher and the principal (if desired) afterward.

Discussion

Goal setting is a key step in solving problems or addressing a need. However, this step is highly recursive. During the goal-setting process, literacy coaches and teachers often gather more information, try out a goal, then perhaps another one, then gather information, and so on. This recursiveness demonstrates that goal setting is not a tidy process. Rather, it has an element of trial-and-error to it, as teachers and literacy coaches work together to find a goal statement that "fits."

I have found four sources of teacher goals:

1. Goals that come from an attempt to solve a problem. I suggest that *problem* is broadly defined to include both the usual notion of a problem as a reflection of a situation that makes one uneasy or dissatisfied as well as the notion that something is lacking, be it a skill, a resource, information, or strategy. In other words, recognition of a problem could mean something is wrong or that something is missing, such as a teacher's knowledge about a topic or strategy for promoting even more growth in students.

2. Goals that come from an attempt to solve a problem that failed. In this case, a teacher previously identified a goal but the goal did not solve a problem as intended. This lack of success is probably due to one of two conditions: either the goal was not the best one for the situation or the goal was a good one but the action plan for reaching it needs to be adjusted.

3. Goals that come from a desire to do something that another teacher has done. A goal like this develops when a teacher visits another teacher's classroom and decides to do what that other teacher has done, or when a teacher attends a workshop or conference and hears about another teacher's work, or when a teacher reads a book or article by another teacher and wishes to adopt a similar strategy, program, or philosophy.

4. Goals that are mandated. Teachers are often told that they must set a goal mandated by their principal, school district, or the director of a particular program (such as Title I or Reading First) of which the teacher is a part. Although research on professional development (Sparks & Loucks-Horsley, 1990) and on human motivation (Leonard, Beauvais, & School, 1995) indicates that individuals learn especially well when working toward goals they have set, such mandates persist and no doubt will continue to persist.

Coaching for Goal Setting

The kind of coaching done to help teachers set a goal varies depending upon the source of the goal. Table 7.1 provides detailed steps for each of the four types of goals. In general, coaches should remember the following when helping teachers to set goals.

- Coaching for goal setting begins with listening and learning. As teachers talk about problems, interests, or dilemmas, they will indicate the source of the goal.

- Encourage teachers to talk about their situations in detail. Use questions suggested in Chapter 6 to further the conversation.

- Invite teachers to state goals. You might also offer your own attempts to state the goals but make it clear that your suggestions are only possibilities and not something to which the teachers must commit.

- Jot notes if it helps you to listen more carefully or keep track of the teachers' situations more accurately. Consider offering visual representations in the form of flow charts, roughly-drawn graphs, or lists of options.

- When in doubt, ask open-ended questions that encourage teachers to describe their situations in greater detail.

- Help teachers frame their goals in terms that focus on their students. In doing so, teachers' goals will be more meaningful and will be easier to monitor for successful implementation. Table 7.2 gives some examples of goals that, through conversation and reflection, are reframed to focus on students.

- Listen for goals that teachers don't really want to meet and don't have to meet. Occasionally, teachers have a sense that they have to do something that isn't required. For instance, teachers may think that they have to use a basal reader for all of their reading instruction when in fact that isn't the case. Coaches who listen and learn, using open-ended questions to further the conversation, can help teachers recognize such goals and move beyond them to more meaningful goals.

- Invite teachers to provide details about what the situation would be like if the goal is met. In this way, teachers can "try on" a goal to see if it will fit. In addition, creating a vision of how the goal will be met enables teachers to move beyond having a problem or dilemma toward a psychological stance of problem solving. Finally, a vision of how the goal will be met will assist in developing an action plan.

Table 7.1. Getting to the Goal

Possible Sources of Goals	Example of What a Coach Might Hear during Information Gathering	Coaching Strategies to Move to a Goal
A problem noted by teacher	"The kids don't make predictions when they read."	■ Ask the teacher to describe the problem in more detail. Get as specific as possible—describe student behaviors, attitudes, products, statements, etc. ■ Learn why the teacher is concerned about this problem. (For example, does it interfere with kids' literacy success, is the teacher concerned about how the children will do next year, or is it something that's "on the test"?) Consider redefining the problem based upon this information. ■ Ask the teacher to describe what will be different if the problem is solved. What will it look like? Sound like? ■ At various points, invite the teacher to try stating a possible goal to see whether it "fits." Suggest you're just "trying it on for size." ■ Alternate between deeper descriptions, further probing of the reason for the teacher's "felt need," and possible goals, until the teacher finds a satisfactory goal.
Previously unsuccessful effort to reach a goal	"I tried to implement DR-TAs [Directed Reading-Thinking Activities] to help the kids predict, but some of the students were afraid to take a risk and make a guess."	■ Review the goal that the teacher was trying to meet with the initial unsuccessful effort and ask if that is still an accurate statement of the teacher's goal. If not, use strategies from the cell above to develop a new goal. ■ If the goal is the same, then gather more information about what worked as well as what didn't work in the teacher's unsuccessful efforts. Again, be as specific as possible and emphasize information about students. ■ Work with the teacher to decide whether the goal might still be met by "tweaking" the previous efforts or whether a new effort should be developed in order to meet the goal. ■ Plan for the next attempt to reach the goal.
Someone else did something the teacher liked	"I read in Linda Hoyt's book that predicting is a good strategy to practice during shared reading."	■ Gather information about why the other's actions are appealing to the teacher. Include questions about whether the appeal is the content, process, materials used (e.g. a favorite children's book), familiarity with the other's work, etc. ■ Help the teacher explore whether she or he needs more experience or information, which could be gathered from visiting the other's classroom, reading more that the other has written, watching a video, watching another teacher who is implementing the idea, etc. ■ Ask what outcome the teacher hopes for if she or he "borrows" this goal. Help the teacher consider how / if the students will benefit or change as a result. ■ Assist the teacher in developing a goal which is (1) her or his own—not someone else's; (2) focused on students, not a method or program.
Mandate from curriculum/ program/ supervisor	"The Reading First evaluator said we need to include more comprehension instruction."	■ Support mandated goals—because neither you nor the teacher wants to be fired! ■ However, identify and work toward the teacher's goals as well. ■ Seek *and* instead of *or* whenever possible. In other words, help the teacher meet goals as well as mandates. ■ Be realistic when teachers see conflicts between their goals and mandates; help teachers cope when they must follow mandates with which they strongly differ. Resisting such mandates is a personal choice but not a coaching duty.

Table 7.2. Reframing Goals

Original Goal Statement	Goal Statement Reframed to Focus on Students
Develop a reading workshop like the one I read about in Sharon Taberski's book (2000).	Develop a reading workshop that will provide students with instruction targeted at their needs or interests
Get my classroom more organized	Provide a variety of reading materials for students to access during independent reading by creating an organized library, book pots, and topical book racks
Learn how to do a running record	Understand my students' in-process reading behaviors by using running records and miscue analyses

Goal setting is foundational to the coaching processes that come after it. Therefore, literacy coaches are wise to take their time and help teachers take their time in developing goals. When goal setting is done well, planning for action and forwarding the action flow smoothly.

Sample Coaching Session: Goal Setting

Coach: When you think about the kind of readers and writers you want your students to be, the kind of teaching you want to do, and the kind of classroom you want to have, what gets in the way?

Teacher: Time! I never have enough time to get to all of the kids in conferences and to do running records and lead guided reading groups. It's just too much to do in an hour.

Coach: Tell me some more about what that's like.

Teacher: Well, we start reading workshop right away in the morning, but I have specials at 9:45 on Tuesdays and Thursdays and at 10:00 on Friday, so we have to get it all done in an hour. I try to do shared reading first and then conference for twenty minutes and then do two guided reading groups in the last half hour. But I never stay on schedule, and it all takes so much longer than I think it will.

Coach: What happens then?

Teacher: Well, I usually end up leaving one of the guided reading groups for the next day, but that has a domino effect, and then I don't get to see all of the groups twice per week.

Coach: Mm hmmm.

Teacher: Also, the kids need my help in between activities—to find new books and figure out what to do next—and I feel so rushed that I either can't help them or I lose my patience with them. I'm sort of embarrassed to say that.

Coach: I hear you. It's hard to want things to go smoothly and then they don't.

Teacher: Yeah. I really thought I had a good plan for reading workshop this year, and I was so excited about it, but now I'm just about ready to give up.

Coach: What is reading workshop like for the students?

Teacher: Well, like I said, some of them are confused. The rest are doing pretty well—they are reading a lot and the guided reading groups do go well when they meet. But I'm worried about those few kids who are struggling.

Coach: I've been taking some notes. Let's see if I have this right: Some parts of the reading workshop are going well, such as the guided reading groups and getting many of the students to read during independent reading. However, you are struggling to fit it all in, a few of the kids don't know what to do during workshop, and you sometimes lose patience. Do I have that right?

Teacher: Also I have a few struggling readers who I'm worried about.

Coach: Oh yeah, I forgot to write that down. Thanks. [*Coach adds to notes.*] OK, when you look at these parts of reading workshop that you want to change, what's the biggest issue for you?

Teacher: I really do think it's time. If I didn't feel so rushed, I could work out the other details.

Coach: What would it look like if you had the time you need for reading workshop?

Teacher: Well, for starters, I wouldn't rush through shared reading. I'd have deeper and more meaningful discussions with students about the poems and stories we share together. Then I'd get more conferences done each day, and I'd get two guided reading groups in each day.

Coach: How much time do you think it would take to do all of that?

Teacher: Well, at least ninety minutes. Two hours would be ideal.

Coach: It sounds like you could approach this situation in one of two ways: You could find more time for reading workshop or try to do less in the time you have. Or a combination of the two depending on the day.

Teacher: I'm not getting enough done as it is! I don't want to try to do less.

Coach: Do you think you could find more time for workshop?

Teacher: I don't know. I'd like to try, but I'm not sure how. We'd have to continue it after specials, and that seems like such a disruption.

Coach: I'd be glad to help you explore finding more time for workshop, if you'd like. And I hear you that you don't want to do less overall, but maybe we could think about doing less on any given day. For instance, maybe you would do conferences only two days per week, but on those days you wouldn't do guided reading groups, and then on the other three days you'd do guided reading but not conferences.

Teacher: That might work.

Coach: Do you think you are ready to state a goal for our work together?

Teacher: Well . . . I'd like to find more time for reading workshop.

Coach: OK, I hear you. What will be the effect on your students if you find more time?

Teacher: Well, my students will be less rushed and confused, and they'll grow as readers because they'll have a better-quality reading workshop.

Coach: How do you think they'll grow?

Teacher: I'll be able to know them better as readers and help them develop new strategies and new interests.

Coach: So could the goal be stated with the students in mind?

Teacher: OK, my goal is to help my students develop new strategies and interests, and to be less confused during workshop time by finding more time for reading workshop and, I guess, rethinking the way I schedule activities in reading workshop.

Coach: I've been writing that down as you said it. Do I have it right . . . ?

INDIVIDUAL CONFERENCE RECORD SHEET

Teacher _____   Grade _____

Coach _____   Date_____

How It's Going:

Items Dicussed:

For Future Discussion:

Next Steps

Goal:

Action Steps:

   Teacher:

   Coach:

Next Meeting:

Bring to Next Meeting:

Distribute:
___ coach
___ teacher
___ principal

8 Planning for Action

Overview

What

- Move from a goal statement to an action plan.

Why

- A plan prepares a teacher to work toward a goal.

How

- Create statements about steps to take, resources to use, and how one will know that the goal has been met.

To Think about During

- How much assistance does the teacher need in thinking about the pieces of the action plan?
- Is the plan broken into steps that make the work easier without focusing on minutiae?

To Think about After

- Does the teacher "own" the plan or is it really the coach's plan?

Black-Line Masters Included in This Section

- **Planning for Action Charts.** These charts will assist coaches and teachers in developing an action plan. The one on the top half of the page provides space for listing steps toward meeting the goal, materials needed, and dates when that step will be completed. The chart on the lower half of the page provides space for listing indications that the goal has been met, tools that will help evaluate the success in meeting the goal, and criteria for determining that the goal has been met. An example of how these charts might be completed, correlated with the sample coaching session that follows, is also provided.

Discussion

Personal traits seem to play a part in how individuals plan to meet a goal. Some people jump right in and start to act, while others think about the goal and develop a detailed plan before acting. Each approach seems useful to some people. However, in the coaching process, at least two people are involved, and coaches usually best support teachers when a plan has been developed which includes steps for meeting the goal, resources needed, a timeline, and methods for determining whether the goal has been met. For holistic thinkers who don't usually develop such a detailed plan, this approach might provide frustration. However, if coaches ask teachers to develop action plans with them in order to facilitate coaching and not to alter teachers' natural way of thinking and doing, teachers usually will agree. Coaches might also assure the more holistic teachers that even if they act in a manner that is not broken into steps, having thought about those steps in advance will probably help further the more holistic action because teachers will be less prone to forget something important.

The coaching task of planning for action is fairly straightforward. After developing a goal together, the teacher and coach then think about what is needed to bring that goal to fruition. A coach who uses the questions for gathering information provided in Chapter 6 will be able to help a teacher do this planning in a productive manner. The black-line master in this section provides a one-page set of two charts on which to keep track of the plans.

If you find at any point that the teacher is having a hard time envisioning steps to meet the goal or signs that the goal has been successfully implemented, return to listening and learning as the teacher describes the problem. When a teacher talks further about a situation, he or she is usually able to return to the ideas for changing it.

A challenge for literacy coaches throughout the coaching process but particularly at this stage is deciding when to make suggestions and when to wait for the teacher to think of something. This decision is largely intuitive, but here are some suggestions to help.

- Use wait time generously in order to give teachers time to think.

- Watch a teacher's body language for signs of "shutting down" communication: folding her arms, turning her shoulders away, or checking her watch.

- If you are unsure whether to help or wait, ask what the teacher would prefer.

- Listen and learn first. Add your suggestions when teachers are running out of ideas.

- When you do make suggestions, frame them as just that: suggestions. Help teachers understand that you are not speaking authoritatively with *the* answer but only offering a possibility.

Occasionally, teachers have trouble seeing a solution and will only be able to see a problem. This happens once in a while to all of us, usually when we have a problem with which we've struggled for a long time. On the other hand, every workplace seems to have one or two people who seem to prefer having problems to having solutions. When working with teachers who are stuck in the problem, give them plenty of time to tell you everything that feels like a limitation toward meeting the goal. Then give them plenty of time to envision the situation if the goal is met. You might even ask, in a neutral voice, "Do you believe that you could attain this in your classroom?" If the teacher doesn't believe the goal is attainable, listen and learn about why this is so and help the teacher decide whether to modify the goal or establish an intermediate goal that will address whatever obstacles will prevent the original goal from being accomplished. It is especially important to complete the second part of the action planning sheet with such teachers. This portion of the action planning sheet provides a chart on which teachers consider what success will look like and how to gauge whether it has been accomplished.

When literacy coaches and teachers have thought through the steps in meeting a goal and have considered how they can determine whether the goal has been met, they will have given thorough consideration to the issue at hand. At that point, taking action should be easy.

Sample Coaching Session: Planning for Action

Coach: When you think about the kind of understanding you want your students to have of biology, the way you want them to use reading and writing to learn, and the kind of teaching you want to do, what gets in the way?

Teacher: The kids won't read the textbook. No matter what I try, they don't do their reading assignments.

Coach: Tell me more, please.

Teacher: With every unit I do, there is a section of the textbook—usually one or two chapters—that the students are assigned to read. I still teach that material, but it helps if the students read it as well. But they just won't.

Coach: Why do you think that is?

Teacher: For a lot of them, the book is too hard. For all of them, it's boring.

Coach: What happens when the students do try to read it?

Teacher: They either give up or lose track of what it's saying.

Coach: Tell me more, please.

Teacher: Well, the book has a lot of print packed on to each page, and of course in science there is a lot of new vocabulary. So the kids often just feel overwhelmed. Also, the book is written, well, like a textbook. You know; it's real dry. Even the students interested in science—the ones who do read it—don't seem to get much out of it. I don't think the book gives enough examples, either.

Coach: What could you do?

Teacher: Well, I end up teaching the chapters in class. But that takes a lot of time, and I want them to be able to read science materials on their own. They'll need to be able to do that in their more advanced science classes and in college.

Coach: What about the kids not going to college?

Teacher: Well, they really need to be able to learn about scientific concepts on their own—because they have a whole life ahead of having to make decisions about products and their health and things like that. If they can't pick up a newspaper or magazine article and understand it, they'll keep making poor choices.

Coach: So tell me if I hear you accurately. You want the students to read in science mostly so that they can develop the skill and habit of reading science materials, because it will help them later, either in future science classes or in life.

Teacher: Yeah, that's it. And also, if they were doing the reading, I wouldn't have to spend so much class time providing instruction, and we could have more and better discussions and projects.

Coach: So in addition to helping students prepare for future learning, in school and in life, you want to spend less time instructing on the concepts that are in the book and more time having class discussions and projects.

Teacher: Right.

Coach: That sounds like a goal. What do you think?

Teacher: Yeah, I think so.

Coach: Can you state it again so I can write it down?

Teacher: Well, my goal is to help students learn to read science materials so they can keep learning about science in years to come and to have students rely less on classroom instruction so that we can do other kinds of activities in class. I guess that's two goals.

Coach: OK, I've written them down as two goals. Which one feels most pressing; which one do you want to work on first?

Teacher: The first one. If the students read materials independently, then the second one will be taken care of, too.

Coach: OK, so the goal is to help students learn to read science materials so they can keep learning about science on their own. Right?

Teacher: That's it.

Coach: When you think about meeting this goal, what does it look like or sound like?

Teacher: Well, the students come to class prepared; done their reading assignments, they can talk about what they've read, and they are interested in it.

Coach: That sounds like an exciting classroom.

Teacher: Yeah. And it sounds like a long way from reality!

Coach: What gets in the way from reaching that goal?

Teacher: Well, again, it comes back to the textbook. It isn't exciting, and the kids can't read it.

Coach: Do you have to use the textbook?

Teacher: No, but it's the only material I have enough copies of for all my students.

Coach: Well, let's see. It seems like the options for meeting the goal are to find some way to interest the kids in the book and help them read it or to find some other materials for them to read. Does one of these options appeal more to you?

Teacher: Well, I wish I could help the kids read the textbook with ease; that would be great. But even then, the book will still be so boring.

Coach: Hmm-mmm.

Teacher: The kids do need to be able to read textbooks if they are going on to college, so I don't want to give up on the book. But I think it would help if there were some other materials, too.

Coach: So I hear you suggesting a third option: Use the book some of the time and use other materials at other times.

Teacher: Yeah, I think that might be workable. Then the kids would all still read the same material some of the time.

Coach: Would you like to work with me to develop a plan to meet that goal?

Teacher: OK, I'll try. But I'm not sure how.

Coach: I wonder if it would help to try this approach with just one unit or one section of biology, to see if it works.

Teacher: Well, I like to keep all of the sections pretty much the same—the kids compare notes, you know. But I like the idea of doing only one unit at a time.

Coach: Do you have a unit coming up that you'd like to use?

Teacher: Well, the next unit is on classification, and we really use the book a lot for that one. Also, I'm not sure if there are a lot of other materials for that topic. But in January, we will begin the unit on ecosystems. That might be perfect.

Coach: In what way?

Teacher: Well, there are some other great materials on ecology and ecosystems. Also, the book is not entirely current, so I've been wanting to do something else with that unit. Oh, but there is a great introductory section in the chapter on ecosystems, and I'd like the kids to read that.

Coach: What would be the first step in meeting this goal?

Teacher: Well, I need to find out what other materials are available.

Coach: How will you do that?

Teacher: I'll look in my own files and talk to the other science teachers. Oh, and there are some excellent resources online.

Coach: How will you select materials?

Teacher: Hmm. Well, the materials will have to be interesting and readable. But also they should build on what is in the chapter—you know, expand on that introductory section but not repeat it.

Coach: So I think I hear you saying that you want to use the first part of the chapter in the textbook and then find other materials that expand upon concepts in that part. Is that accurate?

Teacher: Yeah, and I think there are a couple of other places in the textbook that there are some good concepts. I think I need to decide first what I'll use from the textbook.

Coach: OK, so you will decide what to use from the textbook and then find additional materials. How will you decide what to use from the textbook?

Teacher: Well, I'll pick out the key concepts that we have to teach according to the district curriculum, and then I'll eliminate anything that is not essential or that is hard to understand.

Coach: So it sounds like you have two criteria for what to use in the textbook: First, it teaches an essential concept and, second, it is easily understood.

Teacher: Yes.

Coach: Do you know which essential concepts are in the curriculum? And are there any other sources of key concepts?

Teacher: Well, I'd better check the state standards, too. And although I pretty much know the curriculum, it wouldn't hurt to check back on it.

Coach: OK, so it sounds as if the first step is to review the key concepts that you are required to teach. The resources for that are the district curriculum and the state standards.

(Coach writes information on the Planning for Action Chart.)

Teacher: Right.

Coach: What then?

Teacher: Well, I think then it would be time to go to the textbook and select the concepts I want to have the kids read about.

Coach: OK, then you're going to select sections of the textbook that cover those concepts. And they have to be interesting, right?

Teacher: Yes.

Coach: How do you define "interesting"?

Teacher: Well, the textbook sections should be pretty easily understood so the kids don't give up, and the book should explain with definitions and examples. An interesting resource also uses illustrations or other visuals.

Coach: OK, so you'll find sections of the textbook that are interesting and teach the important concepts. Then what?

Teacher: Well, then I'll find additional materials to use for the concepts I'm not using the textbook for.

Coach: OK, I'm writing step three as finding additional materials. What resources will you use to find those materials?

Teacher: Well, the Internet for sure . . . and my science journals.

Coach: Anything else?

Teacher: Hmmm . . .

Coach: Perhaps some human resources?

Teacher: I could go to the Ecology Action Center downtown and see what they have. Also, I could ask the other science teachers.

Coach: What about the library?

Teacher: You know, our school library is so out of date; there just isn't much there. And I don't like to give the kids materials from the public library because they might lose them.

Coach: OK, then I won't write that down. . . . What next?

Teacher: Well, then I'll plan the unit on ecosystems.

Coach: Do you want to break down that step?

Teacher: No, I've been planning units for years. I don't think I need to.

Coach: OK. What about a timeline for these steps?

Teacher: Hmm . . .

Coach: Sometimes it helps to work backward. When do you want to have the unit planned?

Teacher: By December 15, so I can begin it in January. No, wait. There is way too much going on in December. My daughter is graduating from college, you know.

Coach: Really, already! That went fast.

Teacher: Well, she's graduating a semester early. She took a lot of summer school classes. These kids can't wait to be out on their own.

Coach: It sounds like an exciting December for you. But busy.

Teacher: Yeah. I guess I'll set a deadline of December 1 for the unit.

Coach: OK, then, working backward, when do you want to have the materials selected?

Teacher: Well, I'll need two weeks to develop the unit, so let's say November 15 for the materials.

Coach: OK, you'll find the nontextbook print materials by November 15. What about identifying the parts of the textbook to use?

Teacher: I think I'll work on that soon. Maybe by November 3?

Coach: And the first step—looking at the curriculum and standards?

Teacher: Actually, I'll do that right away, too. Let's put November 3 for the first two deadlines. Then I can sort of go back and forth between them.

Coach: Great. Can you look at how I've completed this first chart and tell me if it looks useful and accurate to you?

Teacher: Let's see . . . uh hmm . . . uh hmmm . . . yes, looks great.

Coach: OK, now we're almost out of time, but could we look at one more thing on this sheet. Here's a chart for thinking about how you'll know if you've met the goal. I find that if I don't think about these issues, I sometimes don't do a very good job of monitoring my progress toward a goal. Could we think about these items?

Teacher: Sure.

Coach: OK, what will indicate that you've met the goal? What are some concrete ways you'll be able to tell that the kids are reading materials about ecosystems?

Teacher: Well, they'll do better on their projects than the classes usually do.

Coach: OK, their projects will show their understanding of ecosystems, right?

Teacher: Yes.

Coach: How will you know that?

Teacher: Well, I have a rubric that I use to evaluate the projects.

Coach: OK, I'm writing that the rubric will be the tool. What will be the criterion to show the students understand ecosystems?

Teacher: Well, I think a twelve or above on the rubric would be satisfactory.

Coach: So if the students get a twelve on the rubric, you'll feel satisfied that they read the material and understand the concepts?

Teacher: Well, wait a minute. That might be a little low. Some students get a twelve by working hard and being creative. I think they need at least a fourteen if they are understanding the concepts.

Coach: OK, I'm going to put down "fourteen or above." What else will show that they have learned concepts about ecosystems by reading about them?

Teacher: The students will be able to participate more in class discussions.

Coach: How will you gauge that?

Teacher: I guess through my observations. That's not very specific, is it?

Coach: Well, observation can be subjective, but it is also one of teachers' handiest tools.

Teacher: Well, maybe the first time through I'll write a few reflective notes on each part of the unit. Then I can make myself actually come up with examples of students participating in discussion, not just assume they are.

Coach: So you are going to write some reflections on the unit and use those reflections to see if students are using key concepts?

Teacher: Yes. I will. It will be a lot of extra work; maybe I could do the reflections for just one or two of my sections.

Coach: Which would work best—one or two?

Teacher: Probably two. You know how every once in a while one section can just be off, compared with the others.

Coach: OK, is there any other way you'll gauge success in meeting your goal.

Teacher: Well, let's see. I guess ultimately I want students to live in a way that reflects they understand ecosystems. You know: recycling, avoiding littering, reusing rather than throwing things away, stuff like that.

Coach: Do you have a way for determining if that is happening?

Teacher: Well, I do ask the students to do a self-evaluation at the end of the unit. It's a form I got at a conference.

Coach: OK, I'm writing that on the chart. How do you determine whether the students are really acting on these concepts? Does the self-evaluation have a score?

Teacher: Yes, it's a holistic evaluation, with overall scores of one to five. I'd say a four or five would be a target.

Coach: OK, four or above on the self-evaluation. . . . Anything else?

Teacher: No, I think that's it.

Coach: Could you look over this second chart and tell me if it is accurate?

Teacher: Yes, it looks great.

Coach: What can I do to help you meet this goal?

Teacher: You've done a lot already with this planning today.

Coach: Can I check back with you to see how you are doing?

Teacher: Yes, maybe after December 1 we could go over the unit and the materials I'm thinking of using.

Coach: I'd be happy to do that. Can we schedule a date . . . ?

PLANNING FOR ACTION CHARTS

Goal:		
Steps to Meeting Goal	**Resources Needed (material/human)**	**Target Date for Completion**
1.		
2.		
3.		
4.		

Evaluating Progress toward the Goal:		
Success Looks Like/Sounds Like	**Tool(s) for Collecting Data**	**Indicator That Goal Has Been Met**

The Literacy Coach's Desk Reference: Processes and Perspectives for Effective Coaching by Cathy A. Toll
© 2006 National Council of Teachers of English.

PLANNING FOR ACTION CHARTS—SAMPLE

Goal: *Increase student understanding of biology by using print materials other than the textbook.*		
Steps to Meeting Goal	**Resources Needed**	**Target Date for Completion**
1. Identify key concepts of unit on ecosystems.	-District curriculum -State standards	November 3
2. Determine whether any of these concepts is presented in an interesting (readable, examples, definitions) way in the textbook.	Textbook	November 3
3. Find materials for those concepts not presented well in the textbook.	-Internet -Colleagues -Ecology Action Center -Science Journals	November 15
4. Plan a unit on ecosystems that includes additional print materials.	——	December 1

Evaluating Progress toward the Goal:		
Success Looks Like/Sounds Like	**Tool(s) for Collecting Data**	**Indicator That Goal Has Been Met**
Student projects demonstrate key concepts about ecosystems.	Student group project evaluation rubric	Scores of fourteen or above on evaluation rubric
Students use key concepts in class discussions.	Teacher observation	Teacher reflective notes indicate observation of students using key concepts.
Students act with awareness of ecology.	Student self-evaluation forms	Students rate themselves at four or above.

The Literacy Coach's Desk Reference: Processes and Perspectives for Effective Coaching by Cathy A. Toll
© 2006 National Council of Teachers of English.

9 Forwarding the Action

Overview

What

- Support teachers as they implement action plans.

Why

- Working toward a goal presents many opportunities for frustration, distraction, and giving up.

How

- Check in with teachers on a regular basis.

To Think about in Advance

- What is a good balance between seeming supportive of teachers yet not nagging them?

To Think about During

- Is the conversation hospitable enough for teachers to reveal their frustrations or doubts?

To Think about After

- At what point will it be effective to check in with this teacher again?

Black-Line Masters Included in This Section

- **Teacher Interaction Chart.** Use this chart to track the interactions you have with individual teachers. Develop additional codes as needed.

Discussion

Anyone who has ever worked toward a goal knows that support is important. Sometimes a person needs support to address obstacles that have gotten in the way of the goal, sometimes a person needs support in the form of someone with whom to share progress, and sometimes a person merely needs support in the form of encouragement. Teachers are no different, and literacy coaches do important work when they provide such support.

Leaders in the field of coaching often speak of forwarding the action to describe the role of a coach in helping others to meet their goals (Fridjhon & Fuller, 2004). In forwarding the action, a coach helps the goal setter keep moving ahead. If good intentions were all it took to meet one's goals, we'd all have clean houses, slender bodies, and balanced checkbooks! Rather, in order to meet goals, a person has to follow through and make good intentions a reality. This is the process of forwarding the action—that is, bringing an action plan to life.

An article in the *Harvard Business Review* recently demonstrated the danger of failing to follow up when changes are occurring. The authors describe patterns of unproductive behavior and thinking that individuals often fall back on just as a goal is about to be met. These patterns enable individuals to return to a more comfortable, albeit less-beneficial, practice and include continually jumping to an option that seems even better, talking about the change without ever acting on it, and becoming overly concerned about getting the change "right" before taking action (Garvin & Roberto, 2005).

The groundwork for successful action is laid when a literacy coach and teacher develop a goal and an action plan. This preliminary work provides a map for forwarding the action. It is tempting, once a goal and plan are developed, to say, "Just do it!" and hope that the plan comes to fruition. However, forwarding the action gives the ongoing support that "Just do it!" fails to provide. Forwarding the action can take three forms: supporting progress, troubleshooting when action slows down or halts, and sustaining the outcome.

Supporting Progress

A teacher may be making good progress toward a goal. In this case, the literacy coach's role is to recognize that progress, to assist the teacher in looking ahead to remaining tasks, and to remind the teacher that the coach is among one of many resources for assistance.

Troubleshooting

On the other hand, a teacher may not be making progress toward a goal. At this point, a coach wants to ask good questions in order to gather information about what is not going well and possible reasons why. The coach and teacher will then want to decide whether the best course of action is to persist with the existing goal and action plan or develop either a new goal or a new action plan. From there, they will proceed with the coaching processes previously discussed.

Sustaining the Outcome

Perhaps the trickiest stage of all in working toward a goal is sustaining success. This is exactly the point where coaching often slacks off, because a coach assumes she or he is least needed when a teacher is successful. To the contrary, a literacy coach performs essential roles at this stage when he or she meets with the teacher to learn about the teacher's success, celebrate that success, inquire about what made the goal work, and in general establish that the coach and teacher are collaborators on a journey that is ending but not over. Beyond recognizing the success and what led to it, the savvy literacy coach will ask the teacher what is needed to sustain that success and will help the teacher optimize the conditions needed.

Forwarding the Action as Part of Literacy Coaching

At its best, forwarding the action occurs in meetings scheduled between the literacy coach and teacher at regular intervals. These meetings have a structure similar to that of other coaching conversations: They start out with a review of the purpose and a focusing question, such as "How's it going?" or "When you think about your efforts to meet this goal, what gets in the way?" The meeting then proceeds with careful listening and learning on the coach's part, as the teacher describes progress toward the goal and obstacles that have gotten in the way of that progress. Then, depending upon which kind of support appears necessary, the literacy coach either provides support for successful progress, helps the teacher develop a plan for addressing obstacles to progress, or supports the sustained successful accomplishment of the goal.

In the hectic day-to-day life of educators, these meetings often seem unnecessary, especially if the goal is being successfully met. With all that is involved in coaching and teaching, forwarding-the-action meetings may not take place because there just isn't time. I'd encourage literacy coaches to recognize the fact that when busy, we tend to make time for what we think is the most important. Coaches therefore need to make time for the stage of coaching that may ensure that action occurs and goals are successfully met.

Some coaches forward the action through on-the-fly meetings. These are interactions with teachers that occur in the school hallway, or on the way to the parking lot at the end of the day, or over lunch. The literacy coach sees the teacher and says, "Say, how are you doing with that goal you set?" The teacher usually replies in a few words. If all is well, the interaction ends there; if the teacher is struggling, the coach makes a mental note to follow up at another time. Such quick conversations are less than ideal, but then again, they are better than nothing.

A better idea is to schedule regular meetings, even if it is for only fifteen minutes. This enables the teacher and coach to sit face-to-face and have a more engaged conversation. Such a meeting also provides greater opportunity for a hospitable environment. I use this term to refer to an environment that optimizes the comfort of both participants—physically by being a quiet space separate from others' activities and emotionally by resonating with calm acceptance (Palmer, 1993). The literacy coach plays a key role in establishing trust by making eye contact, appearing centered and not in a hurry, and giving signals that she or he is listening.

When a hospitable environment exists, teachers and literacy coaches can continue their coaching conversations even if only for a brief time. In this way, literacy coaching becomes even more effective and more capacity building for teachers and coaches themselves.

Sample Coaching Session: Forwarding the Action

Coach: Thanks for taking the time to meet with me. When we met at the end of October, you developed a plan for helping your students read biology materials more successfully. You were going to identify the important and readable parts of the textbook section on ecosystems and include that in your unit, then find additional materials for the remaining concepts. When I checked in with you at the end of November, you had the unit just about planned and felt like you had found some excellent print materials to use. We agreed that we'd meet now, in mid-January, after you had started implementing the unit. So, how's it going?

Teacher: OK, I guess. Last week to start out, the kids read the flyers from the Ecology Action Center, and they certainly found them more interesting than the textbook.

Coach: Why do you think that's so?

Teacher: The flyers are about real life—you know, managing your yard, caring for a household, car maintenance, and stuff like that. A couple of the kids were really interested in the information about dead car batteries and old motor oil and what they do to the environment.

Coach: Sounds like a success.

Teacher: Yes and no. The kids were interested, so that's a big plus. But some of them were not able to connect the practical information with the concepts we were discussing. I'm working on that this week.

Coach: Say some more, please.

Teacher: Well, for instance, the kids liked the practical "how-to" aspect of the flyers from the Ecology Action Center, but they couldn't connect those practical ideas with the concept of an ecosystem of which we are a part. And there is a game on the food chain on the internet, which they all played this week, but they still don't seem to understand why they might change their behavior as part of the food chain.

Coach: So if I hear you correctly, you want the kids to connect science concepts with practical behavior, and they aren't.

Teacher: Right.

Coach: And why do you think that is the case?

Teacher: Well, I'm still relying on parts of the textbook and my class instruction for the concepts, and that means those parts are still dry and sometimes difficult. OK, I try not to make my instruction dry, but it takes so much time if I have to go over everything in the book.

Coach: So it sounds like you've met part of your goal, the part about locating other materials, but that it hasn't gotten you all the way to your ultimate goal of helping the students learn the concepts better.

Teacher: Right.

Coach: So now what?

Teacher: Well, I think I have two choices. I can get rid of the book altogether, if I can find even more materials other than the textbook, or I can just tough it out with the parts of the textbook that the kids have to read.

Coach: And what do you think of those choices?

Teacher: I don't like either. Like I said before, I want the students to have some experience with learning from a textbook, so I don't want to throw it out entirely. But I don't know how toughing it out will help them learn better.

Coach: Here's an idea. Could we look at the literature on content literacy and could I share some ideas about how to help the kids learn more successfully from the book?

Teacher: You mean you have some ideas that you think could help me?

Coach: Well, I'm not sure, but it's possible. I've used some strategies that have worked in my own classroom, and I have some resources with other strategies in them. I think you've already done essential work by paring down the textbook assignments to the key concepts. Now maybe we could plan together some tools to help the students learn more from those parts of the textbook you still assign.

Teacher: I think that sounds great. How do we begin?

TEACHER INTERACTION CHART

Teacher Name	Date	Date	Date	Date	Date	Date	Date	Date	Date	Date	Date	Date	Date	Date	Date

Code: IM = Initial meeting **FM** = Follow-up meeting **NGSM** = New goal-setting meeting **DLP** = Demonstration lesson planning **DL** = Demonstration lesson **DLFM** = Demonstration lesson follow-up meeting **CT** = Co-teaching **CTFM** = Co-teaching follow-up meeting

The Literacy Coach's Desk Reference: Processes and Perspectives for Effective Coaching by Cathy A. Toll © 2006 National Council of Teachers of English.

Section 3: Processes for Group Meetings

Literacy coaches typically alternate between working with individuals and working with small groups of teachers. While many of the processes are the same or similar in either setting, there are some unique strategies for effective coaching of groups. This section will provide processes for forming groups; addressing varying levels of participation, competing claims, and intimidation; and helping group members disagree productively. In addition, processes for book study groups and extended inquiry will be provided. The section begins, though, with ideas for making the processes from Section 2 work with small groups as well.

10 Applying Processes from Section 2

Overview

What

- Use similar processes when facilitating coaching conversations with individuals or small groups.

Why

- Effective coaching with small groups requires strategies for focusing, gathering information, setting goals, planning for action, and forwarding the action.

How

- Follow suggestions in Section 2, with minor modifications for small groups.

To Think about in Advance

- What modifications in my coaching strategies will I make when working with this group?

Black-Line Masters Included in This Section

- **Small-Group Conference Scheduling Form.** This form assists literacy coaches in keeping track of the small-group meetings they have scheduled.
- **Small-Group Conference Reminder Note.** This note serves as a reminder of small-group meetings.
- **Small-Group Conference Record Sheet.** Use this form for keeping track of coaching conversations.
- **Planning for Action Charts.** These charts will facilitate planning the steps in meeting a goal and in evaluating whether the goal is met. Refer to this chart when forwarding the action.
- **Small-Group Interaction Chart.** This chart provides spaces to record the date and nature of each meeting a literacy coach has with a small group.
- **(Refer to black-line masters in Section 2 as well.)**

Discussion

Effective coaching strategies are effective because they support conversation, trust, and decision making. Therefore, these strategies can be used in a variety of settings. In fact, I find myself using them when I am with friends, and I have colleagues who catch themselves using coaching strategies with spouses. Thus, the strategies in Section 2 are applicable in other settings, particularly when coaching small groups. On the other hand, a few modifications might be made for small groups. I've addressed each area below.

Arranging Conferences

Of course, arranging a conference with a small group is more challenging than arranging a conference with only one person. Possible strategies to make such scheduling easier are:

- Rely on e-mail or online calendar programs if your school staff uses them.
- Arrange the initial meeting with a small group yourself, in order to provide your personal touch in contacting teachers. Then, ask someone in the group to be the scheduler for future meetings.
- Never end a small-group meeting without setting the next meeting time and date. In that way, all participants in the meeting can provide information right away about when they are available to meet. In order to facilitate this process, remind small-group participants to bring their calendars to all meetings.

Getting Started

Effective literacy coaches have the same goal for the start of a conference, whether they are interacting with one teacher or several teachers at a time. In both situations, coaches want to set a comfortable tone and establish that they are there to listen, learn, and seek ways to support teachers. Literacy coaches can move the conversation from small talk to a professional conversation by reviewing the purpose of the meeting, based either upon the reason they are meeting with all groups for the first time or the purpose for meeting again that was established when the group met previously.

Focusing

Just as focusing with individual teachers provides the opportunity for literacy coaches to listen and learn, focusing with small groups does the same. The questions that encourage individuals to share also help teachers in small groups to do so. If the meeting is the first one with a group, ask The Question or a variation on it. [For a review of The Question, see Chapter 5.] If the group has met previously, then after getting started by reviewing what you talked about the last time, ask, "How's it going?"

When teachers in a small group tell about how their teaching work is going or describe the obstacles they face, they no doubt will provide more than one problem, interest, or concern. Literacy coaches effectively facilitate the discussion by listing every item that is shared, ensuring that each participant has an opportunity to speak, and calmly bringing the group back to the original question if they digress. After all topics of concern are brought to attention, coaches can then assist groups in setting priorities. After reviewing the list of concerns, a good question to ask is, "When you think about the most pressing concern, which is it?" Members of the group may have more than one concern of high priority, in which case coaches may want to further facilitate prioritizing by stating, "I hear three [or two, or however many] concerns that are high-priority. How can we decide which to discuss first?" This open-ended question will give group members an opportunity to participate in problem solving together.

Gathering Information

As is true with individual teachers, asking good questions is the key to listening and learning in small groups. The same kinds of questions—open-ended, nonjudgmental, carefully-worded questions asked in a neutral manner—work well with individuals or with groups. However, literacy coaches may have a harder time asking such questions when working with several teachers, all of whom have ideas they want to share.

Digressions can be particularly challenging. Although they may seem tangential to the coaching conversation, I find that digressions often help groups to cohere, as members share insights, perspectives, personal histories, and other information. Therefore, I advise literacy coaches to balance the degree to which they direct the group with the degree to which they let the group direct itself. In general, I'd say digressions are helpful if they constitute no more than 30 percent of the conversation. If allowed any more of the conversation time than that, digressions will take up too much of the time.

If, as a literacy coach, you are unsure about how comfortable the group's members are with digressions, or if you are concerned that some group members may not like your efforts to steer the group back to the topic at hand, check in with the participants. You might say something like, "I want to check if all of you are comfortable with the way I am facilitating the group. I want the conversation to be spontaneous and 'real,' but I also want it to be productive. How well am I balancing the two?" Or, more simply, you might ask, "Do you mind if I bring the conversation back to the topic we started with?"

Setting Goals

The process of goal setting is the same whether working with several teachers or with individuals. The patterns of communication may be different, as discussed in the previous section of this chapter and in subsequent chapters. In addition, on occasion the members of a small group start out working together in pursuit of shared goals and then realize that they wish to pursue different goals as individuals. I encourage literacy coaches to honor teachers' preferences in this regard, even if such preferences reflect dysfunction among group members, and to work with the teachers as individuals rather than a group when they request that change. However, savvy literacy coaches will listen for shared goals as they meet with the individual members of the group and, if such mutual goals materialize, these coaches will encourage the group to reconvene or at least to share their progress with one another. Another way to get members of a small group to work together again, if for some reason that is important, is to invite them to engage in a book study group as a team. Sometimes teachers who aren't comfortable in an inquiry-based, problem-solving coaching process together can indeed team to discuss something they have read.

Planning for Action

It is important to plan the steps in meeting a goal and discuss how members of the group will determine whether the goal has indeed been met. The same Planning for Action Charts can be used to do this with a small group as well as an individual teacher. However, the Planning for Action Chart for small groups includes a column to indicate who will do each of the steps in meeting the goal.

Forwarding the Action

The need to forward the action and the strategies for doing so are the same whether one is coaching an individual teacher or a small group of teachers. However, literacy coaches may occasionally wonder whether it is necessary to call the entire group together in order to forward the action. Sometimes, forwarding the action is done "on the fly" as a coach bumps into a teacher in the workroom, hallway, or lunch area of the school. Although these interactions are not ideal for forwarding the action with individuals, they sometimes are the best a coach can manage with a busy schedule. However, with a small group, such interactions actually can be detrimental, for two reasons. First, a literacy coach may get a limited perspective on how a group of teachers is doing if the coach relies on only the teacher or teachers that she or he happens to bump into on the fly. In addition, members of the group need to hear each other speak about their progress in meeting the goal. Among the benefits of working in a group is the collaboration that takes place and the ability of group members to further the thinking of each other. These benefits are lost if coaches fail to reconvene groups periodically.

Additional Challenges of Working with Small Groups

The remaining chapters of this section will address additional factors that literacy coaches should consider when working with groups, as well as processes for two special kinds of small-group work: extended inquiry and book study groups.

Sample Coaching Session: Applying Processes from Section 2

(Note: This example demonstrates what literacy coaches often find, which is that initial conversations with teachers don't always address matters that are directly related to literacy. However, once other issues are attended to, teachers can then work productively in small groups to improve literacy achievement and learning overall.)

> *Coach:* Thanks for making time for me during your planning meeting. As you know, I'm meeting with the seventh- and eighth-grade teams to listen and learn about what you are up to and to see if I can help as you continue to work to help your students achieve.

> *Bob:* Sure. Glad to have you here.

> *Coach:* I guess I'd like to start by asking this: When you think about the kind of teaching you want to do, the kind of learning you want your students to do, and the kind of classrooms and house you want to have, what gets in the way?

> *Theresa:* Scheduling! We have kids going all over the place for special ed. and band lessons and gifted classes. It's hard to teach when someone is always missing from class.

> *Dee:* I agree, but I think a bigger problem is that kids don't do homework any more. No matter how I reward or threaten, I can't get the kids to do their assignments.

Bob: Yeah, but an even bigger problem is that we're not taking advantage of our "house" structure. We never co-teach or plan a unit together. Our courses are so disjointed.

Lonny: I agree with all three of you.

Melissa: Me, too, but I'd add one more problem—not enough books for the kids to read for pleasure.

Coach: OK, I've been jotting down your concerns, and here's what I have. Interruptions to the schedule because students are coming and going; getting students to do homework; the need for more collaboration as members of a middle school house; and not enough books for kids to read for pleasure. Did I get them all?

Theresa: I think so.

Coach: Anything else?

Bob and Melissa: No.

Coach (after a moment's wait time): OK, you have four issues on the table. Does one seem to be more significant than another?

Melissa: I guess needing more books is not as important as the other topics.

Dee: Except, if the kids had more books, they might read more at home, and that's one of their assignments.

Bob: You know, I think if we collaborated more, we could address all of these problems as a team.

Lonny: That makes sense to me.

Coach: So I'm hearing that collaboration might be the first goal to address, and then the others will follow. But I'm also hearing that having more books for the kids to read for pleasure may or may not be important. What do you think?

Theresa: I don't want to give up the issue of scheduling.

Coach: OK, I've heard advocacy for scheduling, collaboration, and more books. I don't hear anyone speaking up for the topic of getting the kids to do their homework.

Dee: That was my topic, and I still think it's important. But I think maybe one of these other ones should come first.

Coach: So three topics are on the table: scheduling, collaboration, and more books. Now what?

Theresa: I don't know . . . I think collaboration is too big a topic. I think if we picked one of the other ones, we would be collaborating, and maybe it could help us build our team-work so we could do more planning together.

Melissa: I agree with Theresa.

(pause)

Coach: I hear two people in favor of collaborating on scheduling or finding more books, and then building more collaboration over time. What do the rest of you think?

Lonny: Sounds good to me.

Dee: I think it makes sense.

Bob: I guess I can live with it, so long as we agree to work toward more collaboration in planning.

Coach: Do you all feel comfortable aiming to collaborate now on either scheduling or getting more books, and then moving on to collaborate in planning in due time?

Various participants: Yes. Yup. OK.

Coach: So what is it—scheduling or getting more books for the kids to read for pleasure?

Theresa: Here's why I'm pushing for scheduling. If the students aren't coming and going so much, we don't have to spend so much time helping them catch up. Then, instead, we could help kids with their assignments during study hall and also have more time for planning ourselves.

Melissa: I think that makes sense. Let's go with scheduling.

Dee: But could we work on the other topics in the future?

Coach: I'll make a note of them as topics for future discussion.

Dee: OK.

Bob: Well, can we really do anything about the kids' schedules?

Dee: Good point.

Coach: If we decide that the schedule is the topic for consideration, we can brainstorm both short-term and long-term solutions. Clearly, a lot of schedules are already in place for the semester. Maybe we could find some other ways of addressing the problem now and strategize how to address it in the longer term as well.

Bob: I can live with that.

Lonny: I'm in.

Dee: OK.

Coach: OK, so the topic at hand is addressing the schedule. Tell me more about what that problem looks like.

Theresa: As I said, the kids are in and out of class all day.

Coach: Does it happen every day?

Theresa: Well, the special ed. kids are in and out every day. Band lessons are in the afternoons on Tuesday, Wednesday, and

Thursday. The gifted kids are pulled on Thursdays, too. That's the worst day.

Coach: Does it look the same to the rest of you?

Dee: Yes.

Bob: Yup.

Coach: How many kids are we talking about?

Bob: Well, we have thirteen special ed. kids in this house who are included for one thing or another.

Coach: Are those kids all included in all of your classes?

Dee: I have eight of them for math.

Bob: All thirteen come to science.

Theresa: I see four for reading.

Lonny: Eight come to language arts.

Coach: And social studies?

Melissa: All thirteen.

Coach: Help me understand something. If these kids are included in your classes, what's the problem?

Theresa: Some days, they don't all arrive at the same time, and they get pulled a lot for testing and other special purposes.

Coach: What about your homerooms?

Theresa: That really varies. Some days the special ed. teachers have them all during homeroom, when they have something they want to do; other days, the kids are all in homeroom.

Coach: What else can you tell me about the kids' schedules? What about band?

Theresa: About half of the seventh-graders are in band, and each one gets an individual lesson every week.

Coach: And the gifted kids?

Dee: They are pulled out in two clusters, one on Thursday morning and one Thursday afternoon. They are supposed to find out what they miss and just take care of it—that's the assumption of the gifted program—but just because these kids are smart doesn't mean they are mature enough to do that on their own.

Coach: Does that mean none of the gifted kids manage to make up what they missed?

Dee: No, I'd say about half of them—there are twenty altogether—do just fine.

Coach: Are there other disruptions?

Theresa: No, I think that's it. Except for absences, of course, but we can't do anything about that.

Coach: OK, this is what I hear. There are four to thirteen special ed. kids included in your classes, and they sometimes come in late or are pulled for testing or other reasons. Also, band kids leave for their individual lessons at various times on Tuesday, Wednesday, and Thursday, and twenty gifted kids are out of classes on either Thursday morning or afternoon. Of those, about ten are not keeping up with what they miss. Do I understand the problem accurately?

Theresa: Yes.

(wait time)

Coach: OK, what problems are caused by these kids' in-and-out schedules?

Dee: It's back to homework. They don't learn what their homework is and do it.

Coach: Is that true of special ed., band, and gifted kids?

Dee: Well, band and gifted.

Coach: OK, what else?

Theresa: Well, it disrupts the class when kids are coming and going.

Coach: In what way?

Theresa: They are noisy. If I'm teaching, they distract the kids from what I'm saying. If the students are working on assignments, they distract the kids from their work.

Bob: And if they are working in groups, the kids come in and don't have a clue what to do.

Coach: Anything else?

Melissa: I don't think the special ed. kids feel like a part of the class when they aren't there at the start. And it confuses them.

Lonny: I've just got to say, I think we are babying these kids. If we lay down the law about what we expect, and we don't give in, we won't have this problem.

Coach: Lonny, you've already suggested a solution. I'll jot that down—just lay down the law. But before we brainstorm other possible solutions, would it be possible to state a goal?

Theresa: What about, "We will have fewer interruptions to class time."

Bob: I still don't think we can control the interruptions that much.

Dee: Well, what about, "We will reduce interruptions if we can."

Theresa: I don't know if that's enough. That doesn't sound like it will make much of a difference.

Coach: I'm looking at my notes from your description of the problem. You said the kids disrupt class time and don't keep track of their assignments. Also, some don't feel like they fit in and are confused about what is happening. Can any of these problems lead to a goal?

Theresa: So you're saying maybe the goal isn't changing the schedule but changing the kids' behaviors?

Coach: I don't know. What do you think?

Bob: I think the schedule has to be addressed. We shouldn't have kids traipsing in and out all the time.

Dee: But maybe we need to work with the kids, too. There is no way we'll fix all the schedule problems.

Theresa: How about a combined goal. Something like, "Reduce interruptions due to special schedules as much as possible, and work with the kids to minimize the problems that occur when they do have to come and go from class."

Dee: I like it.

Melissa: Me, too.

Coach: Bob and Lonny?

Bob: Yeah, I can live with it.

Lonny: OK.

Coach: So here's the goal I wrote down: Reduce interruptions due to special schedules as much as possible and work with the kids to minimize the problems that occur when they do have to disrupt class. Do I have that right?

Theresa: Could you say, "when they do have to come and go," rather than "when they have to disrupt class." We don't want to assume they are disrupting.

Coach: Sure. Thanks. Any other changes?

Theresa: No, I think it's great.

Coach: Everyone else?

Various participants: Sounds good. Sure. OK.

Coach: Would it make sense to think about each part of this separately?

Various participants: Sure.

Coach: Well, then. What about reducing interruptions as much as possible. What would it look or sound like if you succeeded in meeting this goal?

Bob: For starters, the special ed. kids would arrive at the same time as the rest of the kids for every class in which they are included.

Coach: What else?

Bob: And they would come every day—no exceptions for testing.

Theresa: Also, while the band kids have to have lessons, they wouldn't be coming in and out for three days of the week. Maybe kids could be scheduled so they all miss on the same day.

Melissa: Yeah, and wouldn't it be great if that was Thursday, when the gifted kids are out, too?

Dee: But the gifted kids all take band. So that wouldn't work.

Lonny: Couldn't they miss their gifted class instead of our classes?

Dee: Well, they only meet with their gifted cluster one day a week, so probably not.

(pause)

Melissa: Maybe we could get the band teacher to take all of the kids from our house on Thursday, and the gifted kids could go for lessons in the half of the day when they don't have their cluster meeting.

Bob: I like it.

Dee: Excellent.

Coach: I'm jotting these ideas down. What else?

(pause)

Dee: I think we've got the perfect idea. Special ed. kids come on time and stay in class. Band kids are all on Thursdays.

Coach: If that were the situation, would it solve the problems?

Theresa: Not all of them, but it's a start.

Coach: Is it a start you could live with?

Dee: Definitely.

Theresa: Yes.

Bob: I agree.

Coach: OK, how would you get there?

Theresa: Well, we'd definitely have to work with the special ed. teachers.

Melissa: And the band teacher.

Coach: Is that possible?

Dee: I think it would help if we explained that it would be best for the special ed. kids if they were in class from the start.

Melissa: I like that. I'd be glad to talk to Betty and Tim.

Coach: How does that sound to the rest of you?

Dee: Great.

Theresa: Yes, thanks.

Coach: So one step is for Melissa to talk to the special ed. teachers about your concerns for the special ed. kids who are included in your classes, and to ask if these students can get to class on time and not be pulled from classes.

Bob: I'm afraid they aren't going to be able to stop the kids from being pulled for testing. That usually depends upon the schedules of the psychologist, and you know how busy she is.

Theresa: I think that the psychologist does only some of the testing.

Bob: Well, I don't think we'll be able to stop that.

Coach: Is this a matter to address with the entire staff?

Bob: I don't know. Those psychologists are assigned to two or three buildings and don't have much flexibility with their time.

Coach: So what do you want to do about this?

Theresa: What if we talked to the psychologist—got some more information. And talked to the special ed. teachers.

Coach: So if you got more information, you might be able to determine whether anything can be changed?

Theresa: Yeah. Melissa, can you ask Betty and Tim about testing?

Melissa: Sure.

Bob: OK, I'll talk to Juanita about the psychologists' schedule.

Coach: Great. So what I've jotted down is that Melissa is going to talk to the special ed. teachers about having the kids in class on time and all the time, as well as whether anything can be done about the testing schedule. Bob is going to talk to the psychologist about her schedule for testing. Does it make sense to agree to talk about what you've found when we meet the next time?

Theresa: Sure.

Bob: Yup.

Coach: OK, what should I put for a deadline? When can you have this done?

Bob: I don't think Juanita will be back until next week. How about Friday, the eleventh?

Coach: Melissa?

Melissa: That should be plenty of time for me.

Coach: OK, I'll put October 11 as the deadline. Now, what about the band and gifted kids?

Dee: Well, we need to see if the band kids' lessons can be rearranged. That affects the other houses, too, so that might be a whole-staff discussion.

Theresa: Would it help to talk to Eric [the band teacher] about his band schedule first?

Dee: Yeah, I think so. I'll do that.

Coach: OK, Dee is going to talk to Eric about the schedule for band lessons. Meanwhile, should I run this idea past Loretta? She likes to know what's coming up at faculty meetings.

Bob: I think it's too early to bring the principal in. Let's wait until we see what we learn.

Coach: OK, I'll hold off. What else?

Lonny: There's the whole matter of the kids' behaviors when they are missing class. They need to be responsible for what they miss.

Coach: OK, let's brainstorm some ideas for that.

Dee: Well, we do try to hold them responsible now, but it isn't working.

Coach: Tell me about that.

Dee: Well, I deduct points from kids' total scores for the quarter for incomplete assignments.

Theresa: We all do. That's one of our house rules.

Coach: What else have you done?

Bob: Lots of lecturing, which goes in one ear and out the other.

Melissa: The kids have assignment notebooks, and we try to help them keep them up to date.

Coach: How do you do that?

Melissa: Well, I intend to talk with them about their notebooks and how they use them regularly in homeroom. I also want to look at the notebooks with them and make sure they are keeping up with assignments. But I get so busy conferencing with kids during homeroom that I don't get around to the assignment notebooks very often.

Theresa: That happens to me, too. I know we talked about monitoring their use of the assignment notebooks in homeroom, but I haven't done it since early September.

Coach: What about the rest of you?

Bob: It's about the same with me.

Lonny: Guilty as charged.

Dee: I do talk to them, but it feels more like lecturing—in one ear and out the other, as Bob said.

Coach: Have you tried anything else?

Dee: Well, I think we all write assignments on the board, so kids can check there if they are out of class for band or gifted cluster.

(pause)

Coach: Anything else?

Theresa: I think that's about it. Hmm—seems like we could do more.

Coach: Like what?

(pause)

Coach: It doesn't seem like ideas are coming to us quickly. Are there some resources we could turn to?

Melissa: Like what?

Coach: Well, here are some thoughts. We could find out if anyone else in the building has found a way to address this problem. Also, I could look at the literature on homework and on middle school climate and see if there are any suggestions. And maybe we could ask the kids.

Melissa: There's a new one—check with the kids! I like it.

Bob: I would appreciate it if you'd see if you can find any ideas.

Coach: OK. Would you all like to talk to the kids and your colleagues?

Bob: How about if I talk to the kids in each of my sections. That way I'll get to all of them.

Melissa: I think I'd rather have us each do it in homeroom. Those are the kids we know best and who know us best.

Bob: I can live with that.

Coach: OK, I'm jotting down that each of you are going to talk to your homerooms, right?

Various participants: Sure. Ok.

Coach: What about your colleagues?

Dee: Honestly, I don't think anyone has solved this problem, but I'll ask around at lunch time.

Lonny: It's simple. You just lay down the law and tell kids what's expected, and they do it.

Coach: Oh, Lonny, you made that suggestion before, and we've sort of forgotten it. Tell us more.

Lonny: My students know exactly what's expected of them and the consequences. None of this babysitting them.

Melissa: And does it work?

Lonny: Sure. I don't have any problem.

Coach: Tell us more. How do you think you make it work for your classes.

Lonny: I think I come on strong from the first day. They know who's boss.

Melissa: With all due respect, Lonny, I think they're sort of scared of you.

Lonny: (chuckles) I know—that's my aim!

Melissa: Well, it's not mine.

(pause)

Coach: So we have an idea on the table that you just need to lay down the law with the kids. Melissa, I think you are not sure Lonny's approach is consistent with yours. But before we debate that, I need a clearer idea of what it looks like and sounds like in your class, Lonny. Dee has said that her attempt to lay down the law hasn't worked. Why do you think yours does?

Lonny: Well, I think Melissa said it. I make them afraid of me.

Dee: I don't want the kids afraid of me, either. These are seventh-graders with enough on their minds. Teachers need to be people they trust.

Lonny: They trust me. They trust me to mean what I say and say what I mean.

Dee: But do they open up to you?

Lonny: No, and that's fine with me.

Coach: It sounds like the method proposed by Lonny is not something all of you can live with. What do you want to do about that?

Theresa: Lonny has been teaching a long time, and I don't think we should tell him he can't do what he wants to do. But I don't think we should have to do what he does, either.

(pause)

Coach: What do you think of that, Lonny?

Lonny: I can live with it.

Coach: So are you comfortable if we note that your method of getting kids to do their assignments is laying down the law, and it is working for you, but then look for some other methods that the others might be more comfortable with?

Lonny: Sure.

Coach: What else?

Bob: Well, I like our plan to get some more information from professional journals or other teachers.

Melissa: And from the kids!

Dee: Exactly what are we going to ask the kids?

Melissa: I think we need to tell them that it is not acceptable that they are not responsible for the work they miss when they are out of the classroom, and we have been trying to get them to be responsible, but we need to do it better, and we want to ask them what they need.

Lonny: Do you really think that these kids want to be responsible and will tell us what to do?

Melissa: Yes, I do!

Coach: Lonny, I sense from your tone that you don't agree with this approach. I want to remind you that a minute ago some members of this group basically agreed to disagree with you. Can you do the same for them?

Lonny: Yeah, sorry.

Coach: How does Melissa's suggestion sound for the rest of you?

Dee: Well, it's idealistic, but I'm willing to try.

Theresa: Maybe we could tell the kids what we expect—you know, to use your words, what it looks like and sounds like when they are being responsible about missing class—and then ask them what it would take for them to do it.

Bob: I like that. It's more specific.

Dee: We can start with what Melissa said, then add Theresa's idea.

Theresa: And maybe write the kids' ideas on the board.

Dee: Let's give it a shot.

Coach: OK, I'm writing down that you are going to try to talk to the kids about what you expect—specifically, what it looks like and sounds like. Do you want to talk about that now?

Dee: Well, it looks like them all copying the assignments off the board.

Theresa: And asking a friend if they are confused. Coming to me as the last resort.

Melissa: Maybe we should give the kids buddies to help them, you know, to tell them what they missed and explain it.

Dee: I like that idea.

Coach: Do you want to assign buddies?

Bob: Let's talk to the kids first and then consider buddies as an option.

Dee: Good idea.

Coach: OK, so it will look like the kids writing the assignments down and asking friends for help. What else?

Dee: It will sound like them participating in class the next day because they did the assignment.

Theresa: And it will look like them knowing what to do in homeroom when they have time for assignments.

Dee: And doing it!

Coach: OK, the kids will know their assignments, do them in homeroom as well as at home, and participate in class the next day. Anything else?

Melissa: The kids will be standing taller because they are learning and keeping up.

Coach: I'm adding that the kids will feel good because they are doing their assignments. Anything else?

(pause)

Coach: What deadline should we record for the conversations with your homerooms?

Bob: Let's keep it all the same—October 11.

Coach: Is that OK with everyone?

Lonny: Do I have to do this?

(pause)

Theresa: I'm OK if you decide that.

Melissa: Me, too.

Coach: Lonny, do you want to decide?

Lonny: Well, if the other homerooms are doing it, I'll do it, too. It will be interesting to see what they say.

Coach: When should we meet again? If October 11 is the deadline for your tasks, would the following week be possible?

Theresa: How about during our planning time on the sixteenth?

Coach: Does that work for everyone?

Various participants: Sure. Yup.

Coach: OK, I'm recording that we'll meet again on Wednesday, October 16, at 2:15 p.m. At that time, we'll review what you've learned about special ed. and psychologists' testing, any success you've had in asking the special ed. teachers to get the kids to class on time, the response of Eric about band lessons, and information you've gotten from the students about helping them be more responsible. Meanwhile, Dee is going to ask other teachers in the building if they have had any success in getting the kids to keep track of what they miss when they are out of the room, and I'm going to look for ideas in professional journals. Anything else?

Dee: No, I think that's enough.

Bob: Let's do it!

SMALL-GROUP CONFERENCE SCHEDULING FORM

Group (grade level/ topic)	Group Members	Meeting Date	Meeting Date	Meeting Date	Meeting Date	Meeting Date	Meeting Date
1.							
2.							
3.							
4.							

The Literacy Coach's Desk Reference: Processes and Perspectives for Effective Coaching by Cathy A. Toll © 2006 National Council of Teachers of English.

SMALL-GROUP CONFERENCE REMINDER NOTE

Hello,

This is a reminder that we have a small-group conference scheduled for the date and time listed below. I look forward to this opportunity to listen and learn about what is going on in your classroom and to seek ways in which I can support you in your efforts to help students achieve. I also look forward to the collaboration that we can foster in a small group.

See you then!

Teacher's Name:

Names of Other Participants in the Conference:

Date and Time of Conference:

SMALL-GROUP CONFERENCE RECORD SHEET

Group Members _____

Coach _____ Date _____

Grade Level/Unit/Focus of Group _____

How It's Going:

Topics Discussed:

For Future Discussion:

Next Steps

Goal:

Action Steps:

Who	Task	Completion Date

Next Meeting:

Bring to Next Meeting:

Distribute:
___ team members
___ principal
___ coach

PLANNING FOR ACTION CHARTS

Goal:			
Steps to Meeting Goal	**Person(s) Who Will Do This**	**Resources Needed (material/human)**	**Target Date for Completion**
1.			
2.			
3.			
4.			

Evaluating Progress toward the Goal:		
Success Looks Like/Sounds Like	**Tool(s) for Collecting Data**	**Indicator That Goal Has Been Met**

The Literacy Coach's Desk Reference: Processes and Perspectives for Effective Coaching by Cathy A. Toll
© 2006 National Council of Teachers of English.

SMALL-GROUP INTERACTION CHART

Group	Date	Date	Date	Date	Date	Date	Date	Date	Date	Date	Date	Date	Date	Date

Code: IM = Initial meeting **FM** = Follow-up meeting **NGSM** = New goal-setting meeting **DLP** = Demonstration lesson planning **DL** = Demonstration lesson **DLFM** = Demonstration lesson follow-up meeting **CT** = Co-teaching **CTFM** = Co-teaching follow-up meeting

11 Forming Groups

Overview

What

- Facilitate the formation of productive professional learning teams.

Why

- The likelihood of effective literacy coaching is augmented when teacher groups are well formed.

How

- Suggest meaningful groupings and shared purposes to those who are invited to form a learning team.

To Think about in Advance

- What teacher groups are logical because members share goals or interests?
- What teacher groups are logical because the members enjoy working together?
- What teacher groups are logical because all members can meet at the same time?

To Think about After

- Would this group enjoy working together again?
- Can others learn from the way this group formed a team?
- What factors influenced this group to work well together or to fail to work well together?

Black-Line Masters Included in This Section

- **Group Formation Worksheet.** Use this sheet to jot notes about topics around which small-group learning teams might form. Although groups may form for reasons other than a topic of shared interest, literacy coaches who want to form some groups by topic may forget which teachers are interested in which topic. Using this sheet, literacy coaches can jot down the names of teachers who mention interest in particular topics and complete the column about times when each teacher is available in order to facilitate logical teacher groupings.

Discussion

The purpose of coaching small groups instead of individuals is to encourage the development of professional learning teams. Such teams provide numerous benefits for their members, including

- Support as participants struggle with aspects of teaching and professional growth
- Ideas, resources, and perspectives shared among members
- Challenges to growth provided by respectful disagreement
- Increased capacity to learn when in an environment of rich conversations and provocative exchanges.

There are no absolute methods for forming teacher learning groups. In some schools, such groups exist before the coach gets involved. In other schools, schedules dictate which teachers are available to work together. And in some other schools, the creativity of the literacy coach is responsible for successful teaming. A variety of conditions influence the formation of teacher professional learning teams, such as schedules, personalities, interests, grade level or discipline taught, and experience.

I encourage literacy coaches to begin their efforts to form coaching groups by assessing the current situation for two factors. First, look for existing groups or existing opportunities for groups to work together. For instance, some schools provide teachers at the same grade level with shared planning time, which provides a great opportunity for teachers to work together in professional learning teams. Second, listen and learn about the needs and interests of teachers in the school. Look for problems, of course, but look as well for strengths. For instance, science teachers who have succeeded in helping students understand their textbooks might be geared up to form a learning team to find nontextbook print resources for teaching science. In addition, look for interests. Most teachers work alone to learn more about a topic of interest; a literacy coach can serve as the "matchmaker" who helps teachers with similar interests develop a learning team rather than doing the work on their own.

Literacy coaches usually have the easiest time supporting teams that are formed based upon grade level or subject taught. It seems logical that, say, all math teachers or all fourth-grade teachers might want to work together, and such groups probably already collaborate for some purposes, although perhaps not for professional learning. On the other hand, there may be value in helping teachers identify others in other grades or disciplines who share their goals, challenges, or interests. Literacy coaches, who are familiar with teachers throughout the school, are ideal for helping such teachers find each other. As coaches engage teachers in conversations about their interests and concerns, they may want to keep track of the topics discussed, for future reference when forming teams.

An additional task for some literacy coaches will be helping teachers identify broader purposes for professional learning. Coaching conversations typically focus on problems, which is logical given the many struggles presented by the complex job of teaching. However, learning teams often thrive when focused on teacher interests rather than on problems. In addition, literacy coaches may facilitate the formation of extended inquiry teams and book study groups, which are learning communities brought together because of their shared interests or questions. In other words, while a grade-level or discipline-based learning team forms because of mutual teaching responsibilities, inquiry teams and study groups form because the members are interested in the same topic or issue, such as vocabulary development or multicultural children's literature. Later chapters discuss these teams in detail.

Another kind of professional learning team develops because teachers share responsibilities for the same students even though they have different teaching duties. For instance, a music teacher may collaborate with a group of primary teachers to develop ideas for supporting students' print literacy while teaching music. Or a teacher of students with learning disabilities may collaborate with the teachers in a middle school "house" to seek ways to support the students' understanding of content materials in all classes.

An error made by some literacy coaches is choosing a topic for a professional learning team on their own, based upon the coaches' own interests or information they received from a source outside the building, such as a professional journal or conference. These literacy coaches may announce the importance of professional learning related to that topic and invite others on the staff to sign up for a team. Such topics may be timely and relevant to the coaches' perceptions of teacher needs, but unless the teachers are interested in the topic, such efforts are too "top-down" and unduly position literacy coaches as being the experts. In these instances, literacy coaches find that very few teachers sign up for the learning team, or that the teachers who sign up are the teachers who are already collaborating with the coach and highly engaged in coaching conversations.

A better way to introduce a potential topic for a professional learning team is to build interest in the topic first. Literacy coaches can do this by peppering conversations with mention of the topic, sharing information about the topic via a newsletter or e-mail exchange, and providing brief articles on the topic. As staff interest develops, literacy coaches might then mention the possibility of an eventual book study group or extended inquiry group related to it and see what kind of reaction they get. In time, when teachers already have an interest in the topic and know something about it, they will be more likely to want to join a learning team.

An important matter for consideration is the inclusion of nonteaching staff in professional learning teams. In some schools, teaching assistants are automatically included in activities that support the growth of the school's educators, in recognition of the fact that these individuals are important to the students' success. In other schools, teaching assistants are seen as less-than-professionals, as implied by the title "paraprofessionals," and, as such, they are excluded from the learning experiences done by the teaching staff. To me, the first approach makes sense, given that teaching assistants work regularly in classrooms with students and given my belief that inclusiveness is always better than exclusiveness. However, literacy coaches working in schools where the latter is more common will want to think strategically before inviting teaching assistants to participate in professional learning teams. It may help to have conversations with individual teachers prior to inviting teaching assistants to participate in teams, and it may also be valuable to talk with the principal in order to learn any past history or contractual limitations that may influence teaching assistants. Then, too, some teaching assistants may feel awkward joining a group of teachers if they have never done so before, so it may also be helpful for literacy coaches to visit with them in order to discuss the value of inviting all educators to participate in a school's learning teams.

In general, literacy coaches are wise if they facilitate the development of professional learning teams that:

- Include diverse viewpoints
- Address issues that are already in participants' awareness
- Encourage sharing of strengths
- Have enough time to meet
- Are likely to succeed!

Sample Coaching Session: Forming Professional Learning Teams

Coach: Hello Maria, do you have a second?

Teacher: Sure. What's up?

Coach: Well, when we met for a conference last week, you mentioned that you are interested in improving the centers that you use for reading instruction. I have heard the same concern from Donna and LaShonda, so I'm wondering if the three of you would like to form a learning team with me to explore the topic of centers.

Teacher: Hmmm. What would be involved?

Coach: The members of the group can really define what they want to do. I'll facilitate and provide resources, as well as share ideas like everyone else in the group. You might know that we have a couple of these learning teams going in the building right now. One of the teams is reading some articles and developing new instructional strategies for vocabulary development. Another team decided to visit classrooms in other schools and share what they've learned about including kids labeled learning disabled in regular classrooms for reading instruction. Then they are going to develop a plan of their own. So as you can see, the participants on a team clarify their goals and develop a plan.

Teacher: That sounds good, but Donna and LaShonda both teach second grade. How would it work if I was on that team, considering that I am a kindergarten teacher?

Coach: I hear your concern. Certainly Donna and LaShonda's thoughts about centers will be somewhat different from yours, given the difference in age between your students and theirs. On the other hand, I hear them talking about some of the same things you are—finding centers that are meaningful, developing procedures that the students can learn easily—stuff like that. But if the grade level difference is a significant concern for you, do you think one of the other kindergarten teachers would want to join the group?

Teacher: Actually, I think they both might. Would that make the group too large?

Coach: What do you think? Would you enjoy being part of a group of five?

Teacher: Yes, I think that's workable. . . . When do you think we'd meet?

Coach: Well finding a time when all six of us are available will take a little work, but I'm willing to figure that out. Maybe we could find one day a week when we could meet after school.

Teacher: I don't know. Donna picks her kids up right after school, and I do after-school tutoring.

Coach: Can you think of another time?

Teacher: The kindergarten teachers get here early in the morning. Do you think we could meet at 7:30?

Coach: It works for me. I'll check with LaShonda and Donna and get back to you. Meanwhile, could you talk to the other two kindergarten teachers about this idea?

GROUP FORMATION WORKSHEET		
Topic	**Staff Members Interested**	
	Names	**Times Available for Meeting**
	1. 2. 3. 4. 5. 6.	
	1. 2. 3. 4. 5. 6.	
	1. 2. 3. 4. 5. 6.	
	1. 2. 3. 4. 5. 6.	
	1. 2. 3. 4. 5. 6.	

12 Facilitating Disagreement

Overview

What

- Help group members feel comfortable with disagreement and even benefit from it.

Why

- Participants in groups nearly always disagree at some point, so addressing disagreement is essential for healthy, productive professional learning teams.

How

- Make disagreement visible and acceptable, prod group members who agree to disagree but then show discomfort, ask questions to prevent disagreeable members from derailing the group.

To Think about in Advance

- Will some group members feel uncomfortable with disagreement?
- How can I help group members work together even when they disagree?

To Think about During

- How visible should I make group members' differences?
- Do the group members need my intervention or will they address difference themselves?
- Are disagreements fostering or limiting group productivity?

To Think about After

- Is there any "residue" from group processes that I need to address by talking to one or more participants individually?
- Is each group member walking away from this meeting feeling respected and professional?

Discussion

Many of us assume that the basis of working together in small groups is coming to agreement. While agreement can be a pleasure when it occurs, the benefit of small groups often comes when there is a lack of agreement. After all, if all minds think alike, then there is not as much value in working with others. Collaboration provides opportunities to learn from different ideas, perspectives, and experiences. However, such differences often lead to disagreement, and disagreement often makes working in groups uncomfortable.

Literacy coaches play important roles when they help group members recognize differences and even disagree with each other. I find that many people assume that they are comfortable disagreeing with others, until the time comes to do so. For instance, I have worked with teachers in small groups whom I've asked, upon the start of our work together, how they will respond when they disagree with each other. They quickly assured me that that would be no problem—that they'd respect divergent views. Then, when disagreement of any significance actually occurred, group members shifted in their seats, averted their eyes, and became quieter. This was especially true if the disagreeing person had disagreed before or was challenging an idea that the rest of the group was excited about. In other words, groups especially seem uncomfortable with what I call lone outliers.

Lone outliers are those individuals who don't seem to fit into a team. Often, they differ from team members in a demographic characteristic, such as gender or age, as well as in their perceptions, experiences, or opinions. I can only speculate on how characteristics such as gender or age make another feel like an outsider, or like the one in charge, or like the one who has to assert her or his viewpoint. But I'll leave that to psychologists and sociologists. My purpose here is in remarking that observable differences can sometimes combine with different perspectives to create disagreement.

When disagreement in a group does not come from a lone outlier, it often occurs when there is a division among the members. I call this the "Supreme Court Effect" because it reminds me of the current Supreme Court, which has famously split four to five on many key decisions. I work with grade-level teams, disciplinary departments, and entire staffs that seem closely split, like the Supreme Court, and these groups struggle in particular to move ahead. However, members of these groups seem much more comfortable disagreeing with each other, no doubt because there is no one being made to "stand alone."

Whether the disagreement is from one member of a group or half the members, it still creates a challenge for literacy coaches facilitating such groups. I have several suggestions for those coaches.

Don't Pretend Disagreement Does Not Exist

Human nature being what it is, we sometimes want to pretend that what is making us uncomfortable isn't there. We avert our eyes from homeless people, pretend not to notice the fifty pounds our sister has gained, and look away when a parent is shouting at his children in the grocery store. Whether any of these choices are best, I don't know. But I do know that "looking away" from disagreement among teacher groups is not the best route for literacy coaches. If coaches pretend disagreement does not exist when it does, they fail to help the group function more successfully. Moreover, such disagreement may be the very reason why some groups of teachers need a facilitator to help them grow. In addition, if the disagreement is not addressed when it first arises, it will return over and over again. Failure to address disagreement may eventually undo the ability of a group to function productively.

So, how do literacy coaches address disagreement? I encourage them to be prepared for it by expecting it to occur, to be unruffled by it, and to try not to take sides. In the case of the lone outlier, literacy coaches want to avoid both dismissing that person's perspective or giving that perspective undue attention. In the case of a divided group, literacy coaches want to nudge group members to discuss their division, something they may have been avoiding for months or years, like the metaphorical "elephant in the living room" which is an obvious condition that everyone pretends is not there.

There are some communication strategies that can help literacy coaches acknowledge disagreement and make it appear acceptable. One strategy is to make sure the person or persons who are disagreeing know that you heard them. Do this by checking to see that you have accurately recorded their concern in your notes or by asking them to elaborate. Another strategy is to get those who disagree to say something more. Ask them to describe what they are speaking about in greater detail, perhaps by telling you what they see in their own classrooms or what effect their observation may have on students. Finally, label the disagreement as just that, and ask what the others want to do about it. For instance, a literacy coach might say, "I hear that Joan has a viewpoint that is different from the rest of yours. How would you like to consider different viewpoints as a group?"

When disagreement is pointed out to group members, as in the example in the previous paragraph, and when group members are asked how they want to address it, they will rarely say they want to ignore it. Most people just aren't that rude. They may be surprised, because a question about how to address disagreement is not always asked in groups, but they will probably respond. Most often, group members want to agree to disagree. In other words, they want to allow disagreement but don't want to take the same perspective as the person with whom they are disagreeing.

Challenge Artificial Tolerance of Disagreement

As a coach, I usually honor group members' wishes to agree to disagree, but as the coaching conversation continues, I sometimes find that I have to challenge that disagreement. Such instances usually result from my recognition that the group members really aren't speaking and behaving in a manner that respects the disagreement. For instance, teachers may use tones of voice which make their statements seem like put-downs of the opposing view, or they may use body language that indicates rejection of an outlier. At such points, I will remind participants of their previous statement that they wish to agree to disagree and check in if that's still the case, or I'll simply check in again by asking the group how they want to address their feelings of disagreement with each other. This is a risk, because it places the literacy coach in the position of challenger. However, I find that helping groups manage their disagreement is important enough that I will take a risk. I do make such observations or questions in as neutral a voice as possible, and I often explain that I'm emphasizing the need to address disagreement because I want the group to be successful.

Don't Attempt to Erase Disagreement

Addressing disagreement does not mean erasing it. When members of a group face their disagreement, they are wise to maintain it. Research on group functioning in work places recognizes that disagreement is productive (De Dreu & De Vries, 1997). As pointed out at the beginning of this chapter, disagreement represents divergent views, and divergent views bring richness and variety to collaborative efforts. In fact, organizational psychologists suggest that a sign of an organization's health is its ability to tolerate the lone outlier (Nemeth as cited by Achinstein, 2002).

Instead of undoing disagreement, productive learning teams pay attention to it. They use the information, experiences, or values of those who differ to gain new perspectives, but they also pay attention to their own discomfort with the difference. Such discomfort can provide deeper insight into one's own views and reactions. For instance, if a group member suggests that teachers at a grade level do an integrated unit on baseball, and I find myself bristling, I might want to pay attention to my negative reaction. If I did, I'd probably recall that when I was in elementary school, I was overwhelmed by math story problems that related to baseball. Such problems often involved figuring averages and used terms like *RBI* (runs batted in), which I didn't understand. If I think about that as an adult in a professional learning team, I might recognize that my own reaction to baseball story problems doesn't mean that students in present times don't understand baseball. (When I was growing up, many girls didn't pay attention to baseball, especially baseball statistics. I wouldn't assume that was the case with the students in the school where I was working as a coach, although I might ask questions to check it out.) Then again, my own confusion about baseball might make me more sensitive about introducing topics that my students know little about. Such reflections on my own feelings of difference with a colleague can produce insights and further my thinking.

Literacy coaches can play important roles in helping members of a group tolerate difference and pay attention to their own reaction to it. Again, good questioning is key. Some questions coaches might ask include:

- Why do you think you have such differences among yourselves?
- What is behind your response to that idea?
- Can you think of a reason why that idea makes sense to someone else even if it doesn't make sense to you?

Address Attempts to Derail the Group's Productivity

Sometimes an individual, usually a lone outlier, will repeatedly attempt to interfere with the group's work. These individuals will continue to offer disparate views even when the other group members have recognized that they disagree with the outlier but have chosen to respect that person's different perspective. Or, these individuals will disagree so often that one starts to suspect they are disagreeing for the sake of being disagreeable.

Literacy coaches face a challenge when attempting to address disagreements that appear designed to derail the group's progress. In such situations, savvy coaches maintain politeness and a neutral demeanor in interacting with the person who is being disagreeable. However, they also draw a boundary at the point of letting that person hinder the group's productivity or treat group members rudely. A few strategies they use:

- They challenge vague remarks made by the person who is chronically disagreeable by asking that person to say more.
- They repeat the goal and/or the agreed-upon process that will be used as a reminder to the disagreeable person.
- They acknowledge that the person disagrees but ask if he or she can live with what the group has decided. In this way, literacy coaches acknowledge alternate perspectives but remind participants that members of a group sometimes have to live with a decision that they don't like.
- They establish a boundary of what is acceptable if it is necessary to stop a group member from being verbally abusive.

Usually it is best to talk to a person who seems to be antagonistic to the group outside of the group's meetings. In that way, literacy coaches can listen to and learn about that person's concerns, without fear that other members will be upset, and they can express their own wish to have the group collaborate even in the face of difference. If in a particular situation a group member maintains an interest in working against the group's efforts, literacy coaches may be wise to ask that person to cease participating with the group. I suggest this option only after all else has failed.

It is always a risk for literacy coaches to take a problem to their principal. Coaches don't want to be perceived as tattletales. However, a literacy coach may have no other choice but to get help from a principal if a group member violates basic principles of appropriate conduct. Go to the principal if you must, but do it rarely.

Literacy coaches play important roles in influencing the tenor of group work. When they are fair, open-minded, and respectful, they can usually approach disagreements in a manner that will help the group move ahead and even benefit from differences among its members.

Sample Coaching Session: Facilitating Disagreement

Coach: We agreed at the last meeting that we'd discuss vocabulary challenges that students encounter in their math textbook. However, first I'd like to ask, how's it going?

Bart: I've been having the kids write their own story problems, like we talked about last time, and it has helped. They are starting to be better able to see the patterns of problems and questions.

(pause)

Coach: What else?

Janelle: Well, I think if we do some work on the way familiar words have unexpected meanings in math, then the kids will be doing much better. I'm ready to dig in!

(pause)

Coach: What about you, Bonnie?

Bonnie: I just think this is an awful lot of work for math teachers. If they learned to read in English class, it wouldn't be a problem for us. It's like we are doing the English teachers' work.

Coach: Say some more about that, please.

Bonnie: I just don't think this is our job. I teach math, not reading and writing.

Coach: I hear your strong feelings, Bonnie. What do the rest of you think?

Janelle: I don't teach math. I teach ninth-graders. And these strategies help them learn math better.

Bonnie: I've taught for fifteen years, and it wasn't like this when I started out. Why should I start now?

(pause)

Coach: Bart, do you have any thoughts?

Bart: I guess I agree with Janelle. I wish I didn't have to take the time to do this extra stuff, but if it helps, I guess it's worth it.

Coach: So I hear there's a pretty big disagreement among the three of you, and I'm wondering how we proceed.

Janelle: Well, I respect Bonnie's opinion and everything. I just want to be able to do the things I want to help my students.

Bonnie: This is just such a waste of time! I have tests to grade.

Coach: The last thing I want is for these group meetings to be a waste of time. I want them to support you in doing the teaching you want to do. What would it take to make this meeting feel valuable?

Bonnie: Well, we could grade tests together.

Coach: My role is to support capacity building, to help you grow your strengths and develop new ones. I'm not sure that grading tests would do that.

Bonnie: I was just kidding. I guess it's fine with me if we keep going. I'll just listen.

Coach: Your participation is valuable, like the participation of all of us. My wish is that you'd continue to be involved in the discussion, even if you disagree.

Bonnie: Well, I'm just holding everyone up. Let's continue.

Coach: OK, I hear that two of you are ready to talk about terms used in math, but one of you isn't. What should we do now?

Bonnie: No, really, let's just continue.

Coach: Is it helpful to your professional growth if we talk about vocabulary used in math?

Bonnie: Well, it might be. Let's try.

Coach: OK. Can you all tell me some more about this challenge? What causes a problem when the students read familiar terms in unfamiliar ways?

Bart: Well it confuses them. They think a word like *ray* means a sunbeam or a fish, not a kind of line.

Janelle: Or that a prime number is a really important one!

Bonnie: You aren't serious, are you?

Coach: Is that the question you really want to ask, Bonnie?

Bonnie: Yes, it is. I can't believe they think those words confuse the kids.

Coach: Bart, Janelle, do you want to respond?

Janelle: Well, I do think kids get word meanings confused. Maybe those examples aren't good, but it happens.

Coach: Do you ever notice that your students get the meanings of familiar words confused with their meanings in mathematical concepts, Bonnie?

Bonnie: No, I don't.

Coach: This discussion is centered upon that premise. I'd suggest that we build on that. Can you live with that, Bonnie?

Bonnie: OK.

Coach: So, what would it look like if you solved this problem . . . ?

13 Addressing Varying Levels of Participation

Overview

What

- Facilitate groups in a manner that makes participants feel comfortable being involved in differing ways.

Why

- Individuals have different styles of participating in different groups.

How

- Honor the range of participation styles and think carefully before challenging any. If you do challenge, do so outside of the group's meetings.

To Think about During

- Are all group members engaged in a manner consistent with their own style?
- Am I responding to participants according to their need or mine?

To Think about After

- Did all members of the group participate? How do I know?

Discussion

Individuals have different ways of participating in groups. This seems like a commonsense notion, yet it is one that leaders sometimes forget. Perhaps because leaders themselves tend to participate in an active, visible, and audible way in many groups, we tend to expect others to participate similarly. However, some individuals are rather quiet when they are actively participating, taking it all in and reflecting deeply but speaking little. Others like to sit in the least visible place in the room or around the table, participating but hardly being seen.

I encourage literacy coaches to be cautious when determining whether a group member is indeed participating and benefiting from being in the group. Rather than applying their own style of group involvement as the standard, literacy coaches are wise to consider many styles. Members might be quiet or talkative, leading or standing to the side, at the head of the table or the far end. The key is not how much of a person is inserted into the group's activities but rather how much of the group is inserted into the person. In other words, if a person gets something out of being in the group, then they are probably participating at an adequate level.

If literacy coaches have questions about whether certain teachers are comfortable with their levels of participation in groups, the best thing to do is to ask them—but ask outside of a group meeting, to save the teachers from possible embarrassment. Typically, quiet participants do indeed feel that they are getting something out of their participation, and usually literacy coaches will be assured by checking with them.

On the other hand, noisy, overly-talkative group members can be more of a problem. Teachers who dominate groups are usually limiting the effectiveness of that group because the diversity of viewpoints is probably not being heard. Again, literacy coaches are wise to take up this matter with talkative participants outside a group meeting. A good way to approach this situation is to be candid but kind. Try saying something like,

> I notice that you speak a lot during our group meetings, and I'm wondering how that is working for everyone. What do you think?

When asked a question like this, most teachers will apologize and will vow to speak less. As a coach, I often then tell the teacher that I am sincere in saying I'm wondering how it works for everyone. If I ask a question, I am usually sincere in asking it, and I truly will want to know in this instance how the teacher thinks the group is working. My hope will be that, with this clarification, the teacher and I can truly reflect on the matter.

If you talk to a teacher about her or his level of participation outside of the group, and a problem persists, you may want to try one of these strategies.

- Ask the group to do a self-evaluation. Perhaps this will consist of two or three questions that you ask group members to answer in writing. You then collate the responses and share them with the group at the next meeting.

- Ask the group to reflect upon what is working well for them and talk about that. Then ask them how to maximize the components that work well.

- Offer to create a "fishbowl" activity with another group. While one group is meeting, the other group observes and provides feedback. Then, when the other group meets, the first group observes and provides feedback.

- Invite a "critical friend" to visit the group and provide feedback. The members of the group may want to select the person who serves as critical friend.

Helping members of a professional learning team feel comfortable with their individual styles of participation is rather easy to do. However, literacy coaches and others may forget that there are varying ways to participate comfortably. This is one more area where a coach can be responsive to the wonderful diversity found in any group.

Sample Coaching Session: Addressing Varying Levels of Participation

(Note: This conversation is conducted outside of the group meetings.)

Coach: Hi, Lois. Thanks for giving me a few minutes of your time.

Teacher: Sure. What's up?

Coach: I have enjoyed working with you and the other fourth-grade teachers in our professional learning team. I wanted to check with you to see how you think the team is doing.

Teacher: Great. I really enjoy my colleagues, and I'm glad we're meeting.

Coach: I notice that you speak a lot more than the others. How is that working for you?

Teacher: Well, you know I like to talk. What? Am I talking too much?

Coach: Not for my sake. But as a facilitator, I'm always asking questions in my head. One of my questions is: How is the fact that one member talks more than the others working for all members of the group? And because I'm not sure, I thought I'd get another opinion. What do you think?

Teacher: Gosh, I'm embarrassed if I'm talking too much.

Coach: I'm not saying that. I'm asking you for your thoughts. It seems like everyone on the team is getting something out of our work together. Do you think anyone wishes they had a chance to say more?

Teacher: Gee, I think they'd speak up if they had more to say. Well, wait a minute, maybe not Lynette. She's so young; sometimes I think she's afraid to say what's on her mind.

Coach: Do you have any advice for me about how to help her?

Teacher: Hmmm . . . Maybe I'll talk to her about what we've been discussing at the meetings and get her ideas one-on-one. Then I'll encourage her to share them when we are all together.

Coach: That sounds great. Anything else I should consider?

Teacher: Well, maybe if I talk too much, you could give me the evil eye or something!

Coach: Well, again, I don't know if you're talking too much. Maybe when you are talking, I'll watch Lynette to see if she looks like she wants to say something.

Teacher: That would be good. And, you know, I'm going to watch myself a bit more. I do think I could talk a little less.

Coach: Maybe we can both watch the levels of participation when we meet next week, and touch base briefly afterward to share impressions.

Teacher: Great. I'm glad to help. And thanks for talking to me about this.

Coach: No problem. Thanks for your reflections.

14 Addressing Competing Claims

Overview

What

- Move arguments about what will or won't work to a level where group members are able to think more deeply about support for such claims.

Why

- Literacy coaches can help teachers consider the bases for their claims and evaluate the relative merits of those claims. Literacy coaches can help teachers become informed "consumers" of data and research.

How

- Invite teachers to support claims and talk about the varying kinds of support.

To Think about During

- What processes will help members of this team decide which claims make more sense to them?
- What additional resources would help participants consider the claims being made?

To Think about After

- Did all members of the group feel that their claims were treated with respect, even if they were disagreed with or contradicted?

Black-Line Masters Included in This Section

- **Overview of a Research Study.** Use this form to note important details about research studies that are being discussed or argued about by members of a professional learning team.

Discussion

When two or more people gather for a discussion, chances are they will have different perspectives on some topics. Disagreement in general was discussed in the previous chapter. This chapter addresses a specific kind of disagreement: competing claims.

Competing claims occur when two members of a professional learning team make opposing statements based upon information each person says is correct. These claims are usually based upon one of two sources: research or experience. The latter source includes experiences teachers have with their own classrooms, as when a teacher declares, "Well, that's fine in some schools, but it would never work for *my* students."

When literacy coaches are confronted with competing claims, they may want to first help the members of the group feel comfortable with the disagreement by acknowledging the routine nature of such claims. For instance, a coach might say, "It's interesting, isn't it, that so often in education we find opposing viewpoints or practices being supported by different studies."

Coaches are then wise to use the disagreement as an opportunity to help the teachers in the group determine how they choose to believe what they do. They can accomplish this task in several ways.

Competing Claims about Research

A simple response to disagreements among teachers about what "the research says" is to invite teachers to bring the research to the next group meeting. When they do, literacy coaches can help group members think about why two pieces of research would support opposing conclusions. This requires coaches to be comfortable reading and interpreting research. Coaches who aren't informed "consumers" of research themselves may want to ask a colleague for help in making sense of the studies, and then they may want to set a goal for themselves of learning more about research. Literacy coaching frequently requires a familiarity with research, and coaches are wise to take a course, read some books, learn from colleagues, or in some other way develop a greater ease with research, if they don't feel that ease already.

Beyond understanding the structure of a research study, kinds of research methodologies, and some basic statistical and ethnographic terms, literacy coaches will be helped by a bit of epistemology, or understanding of knowledge claims. A concept to consider is the notion that research can "prove" anything. Often, those unfamiliar with research believe that it does indeed provide proof, when in fact research at its best does nothing more than support a theory or hypothesis. This support may be strong, if the research provides a great deal of evidence in support of a claim, or weak, if the research supports the claim a bit, but it is never proof. Coaches aware of this concept can help teachers understand that it isn't helpful to look for proof of a position.

Another epistemological concept to consider is the idea that there is an objective determiner of the truth. This notion is disputed a great deal these days by thinkers who believe that what one decides to be the truth depends upon what one uses as a barometer of that truth (Barrett, 1991). For instance, it may seem true to some teachers that a student who learns differently has a learning disability, whereas to other teachers it seems true that that student is a highly creative genius. In some settings, arguments might persist for a long time about which claim is accurate based upon *the truth*. In other settings, though, a different approach is taken. Rather than try to discover *the* truth about this student, teachers may discuss what their determination of truth is based upon. For instance, one teacher may say that her claim that the child has a learning disability is based upon test scores and the federal definition of a child who is eligible for services in a special education program. Another teacher may say that his claim that the child is a genius is based upon his reading of biographies of famous people who have been declared geniuses in various lines of work. The task before the teachers then becomes not so much a matter of deciding which description of the student is true but, rather, which description of the student is based upon more reliable information (and perhaps the conclusion is neither!).

Literacy coaches who take the epistemological stance that knowledge claims are made by more- or less-reliable evidence, not by a quest for the truth, may want to help group members consider the evidence behind their claims in this way. If the source of the disagreement is educational research, literacy coaches still need to know how to make sense of research in order to help teachers evaluate the evidence for its conclusions. However, if the knowledge claims are made by teachers about their own experiences, coaches can take a slightly different approach.

Competing Claims about Experience

When teachers in a professional learning group make claims based upon their experiences, literacy coaches first might do what they always do: listen and learn. In these instances, coaches may want to say something like, "It's interesting that you disagree about this and that you base your disagreement on your own experiences. Can you each tell us more about what those experiences were like?" As each teacher responds, group members, including the teachers who disagree, will often recognize that the competing claims do indeed have validity, but only in a particular situation or under particular conditions. Often, the competing teachers sheepishly recognize that they probably both are speaking a truth about their respective experiences. For instance, one teacher may claim that parents of poor children never come to parent-teacher conferences, whereas another teacher may claim that such parents always come to conferences with her. In explaining their claims, the first teacher realizes that the one time none of the parents of poor children came to conferences occurred when conferences were held only during the day and parents in service-industry jobs were unable to get away from work. On the other hand, the teacher who had every parent of poor children in attendance at conferences realizes that all parents came because she included the students in the conference and gave a set of markers to each child who was there.

If teachers don't recognize the uniqueness of the situations that lead to their claims, then literacy coaches might ask something like, "How could it be that you have drawn different conclusions from your experiences?" As the teachers consider the matter further, they will almost certainly admit that their claims are relative to individual instances and nothing more.

On the other hand, claims made by teachers based not upon their own experiences but upon more general notions about reality may be more difficult to address. These claims are those about what might work "for my kids" or "when the students get to high school," or "for all English language learners." When these claims are made, literacy coaches may want to ask the group to restrict their claims to those they can support with their own experience or documented experiences of others. The more factually this is stated, the better. For instance, a literacy coach might say, "I appreciate your idea. However, in situations where two of you are making competing claims, we as a group will be on the spot to try to determine which claim we agree with. In order to make that process easier, I'd like to ask that we stick to claims based on our own experiences or on the documented experiences of others. It's just too hard to consider the validity of a claim made about what might happen to your students."

The keys to successfully addressing competing claims are the keys to effective literacy coaching overall: listen and learn, ask questions to prompt reflection and decision making, and speak with respect to all.

Sample Coaching Session: Addressing Competing Claims

Coach: OK, we have two ideas on the table as possible solutions to the problem of students not doing their homework. One is to eliminate homework all together, and the other is to use a system of rewards and punishments. What are your thoughts?

Carlos: Using a behaviorist system of rewards and punishments won't work. Behaviorism just doesn't work.

Terry: Well, that would be a surprise to a couple of generations of behaviorists who have gotten people to do all sorts of things.

Carlos: There's this great book, *Punished by Rewards*, by Alfie Kohn, in which he explains why rewards don't last and why it eventually doesn't work to use them.

Terry: I have rewarded kids a lot, and it has helped tremendously. They do their homework; they participate in Jump Rope for Heart. . . . Heck, my own kids do their chores because of a reward system.

Paulina: Carlos, why do you think it would be better to just not give homework?

Carlos: I read an article about a school that was doing that. It was a middle school, too, and the teachers just stopped fighting the fight. They help the kids practice what they are learning in study halls and homerooms, I think, but they don't expect it at home.

Paulina: And it worked?

Carlos: Yeah, they said it made things much better. Kids were no longer getting low grades just because they didn't do their homework. They felt more successful and liked school better.

Coach: It sounds like we have competing claims here. That's not that surprising—it happens all the time in education, doesn't it? The challenge is to figure out what to do about them. Terry and Carlos, you've each told us a little about why you support one of these ideas. Can you say more about the evidence you have for your claims?

Terry: Well, scientists have been using rewards and punishments all the way back to Pavlov and his dogs.

Carlos: That wasn't a case of rewards and punishments. It was conditioning.

Terry: And Skinner—he proved that rewards work.

Carlos: He didn't prove anything. He raised his kid in a box!

Coach: I know you're having fun here with this argument, guys, but could I ask you to help the group by sticking to what you know about the evidence for your own claim? At least for starters.

Carlos: OK, sorry.

Terry: Well, I guess I don't have one single study or anything. I just know that there is a lot of research to support rewards and punishments, and I know it has worked for me.

Coach: OK, I hear, Terry, that your evidence for your claim is that there is research that has supported rewards and punishments, and that it has worked for you. Has any of that research or have any of your experiences related specifically to getting middle school students to do their homework?

Terry: Well, I don't know of any research specifically, but I would guess it is out there.

Coach: OK, thanks for your candor. Carlos?

Carlos: I base my argument on what I know about this other school that eliminated homework and how happy they were with the success. Also, it makes sense that if we've tried everything to get the kids to do their homework and it still hasn't worked, maybe we should look for a different approach.

Coach: Thanks, Carlos. Do you have that article?

Carlos: It's at home on my desk.

Coach: Would it be fair of me to say that the evidence for both of your claims is not real specific right now?

Carlos: Well, I can bring in the article.

Coach: I hear you. And that's where I'm heading. Would it make sense for us to get some more information before making a decision about your competing claims? Maybe you could find some research to support rewards and punishments, Terry, and you could bring the article and see if you can find more information about schools that eliminated homework, Carlos.

Terry: That makes sense. I'm not a real good researcher, though. Could you help me?

Coach: Well, there are four of us. Should we split the job? I'll help with a search for research on rewards and punishments to get kids to do their homework, and, Betty, would you help Carlos investigate the school he's talking about or other schools that have eliminated homework?

Betty: Sure. Glad to.

Coach: I'd also like to suggest that we think particularly about the evidence that demonstrates whether these methods work or not. We'll probably find evidence to support both, so we'll need to look at the nature of that evidence in order to make a decision.

Terry: Makes sense.

Coach: Anything else?

Betty: Well, I'm interested in the long-term evidence of kids' academic achievement.

Carlos: Yeah, I like that.

Coach: OK, that's evidence we'll want to especially look for. What else?

Carlos: I think that's all.

Terry: I'm good.

Betty: Yup.

Coach: OK, when will we meet again . . . ?

OVERVIEW OF A RESEARCH STUDY

Title: **Author:**

Source: **Publication date:**

Publication location (if appropriate):

Page numbers (if appropriate):

Kind of research:

Research question or hypothesis:

Summarize methods used:

Sources of data (study participants, documents, sites, etc.):

Summarize findings:

Summarize conclusions:

Your reaction:

The Literacy Coach's Desk Reference: Processes and Perspectives for Effective Coaching by Cathy A. Toll
© 2006 National Council of Teachers of English.

15 Addressing Intimidation

Overview

What

- Intervene when a member of a professional learning team is attempting to intimidate other members.

Why

- No one should have to participate in a group in which intimidation is occurring. Intimidation limits a group's productivity and diminishes the dignity of those participating.

How

- Talk to the intimidating group member, usually outside of the group meeting. During the meeting, reduce the group member's fear or sense of powerlessness.

To Think about in Advance

- Why would intimidating behavior seem "right" to this group member?
- How can I increase the feeling of power and control of the intimidator without lessening that feeling in other group members?
- Am I going into this meeting feeling as centered as possible?

To Think about During

- Am I behaving respectfully toward the intimidator, even if I don't like his or her behavior?

To Think about After

- Can this group continue to work together at this point?

Discussion

An earlier chapter discussed disagreement among group members. It began by stating that disagreement is to be expected when people work in groups, and it can even be a sign of a healthy group when participants comfortably disagree. Intimidation, however, is not a normal part of group work, and it is not healthy. While disagreement, even vociferous disagreement, is targeted at the ideas being debated (although it may also be targeted at something else, such as a feeling that one is being ignored), intimidation is always targeted at other members of the group. Intimidation is an attempt to lessen the feeling of power held by one or more group members, carried out by using verbal and visual cues, with the outcome that intimidated members of a group participate less actively.

When group members intimidate others, they typically use one of these tactics:

- Saying something that sounds so knowledgeable that other group members feel ignorant by comparison
- Saying something that makes the speaker seem to have insights garnered from unique experiences that other group members have not had
- Using a tone of voice that sounds bored or surprised by the supposedly simple-minded statements being made by other group members
- Displaying body language that implies impatience or imperiousness, such as tapping one's fingers on the table, rolling one's eyes, or tossing one's head

If, in response to a group member's intimidation, the other participants say little or challenge less, the intimidator has accomplished his or her goal. This is the damage done by intimidation: it reduces others' feelings of self-efficacy and eliminates the richness of diversity from the conversation.

I discourage literacy coaches from "playing psychologist" and assuming they know what is going on in another person's mind. However, I do encourage coaches to use their knowledge of human nature to reflect upon behavior patterns that are fairly common. The purpose of reflection in the case of an intimidator is to gain perspective on how one might effectively respond to intimidation.

I hope I am not an intimidator when I work in groups, but I'm human enough that I can recall times when I was tempted to behave in an intimidating manner. When I reflect upon those times, I was feeling like I had *less* power than others, or I was feeling fearful that I was not going to have enough control in the matter being discussed. My hunch is that these feelings of less power or fear may be common among others, too, when they have an urge to intimidate. This information can be helpful to literacy coaches as they facilitate professional learning teams.

Even when intimidation occurs, there may be time to turn the meeting around and create an environment in which the intimidator will alter her or his behavior without having it addressed directly. In order to effect such a change, literacy coaches will need to act quickly because, if intimidation continues for more than a few minutes, it will be difficult for the intimidator to stop. The tactic coaches want to try early in the intimidation event is to try reducing the feeling of powerlessness or fear that the intimidator might be experiencing. To reduce intimidators' feelings of powerlessness, help them see that they do indeed have power. In any situation, all participants have power to a greater or lesser degree. For instance, in professional learning teams, literacy coaches often have the power to start and to facilitate the meeting. However, meeting participants could be visiting about something else as they enter the meeting room and continue talking about that topic even when the coach asks them to think about the purpose of the meeting. This is just one example of the many ways that power "circulates" through a group meeting (Foucault, 1980). Not everyone realizes, though, that power functions in this way among groups. Some people mistakenly believe that power can be "had" by one person in a group, if the others allow that person to "take" it from them. In other words, some people believe power is a commodity in limited quantity that must be harvested and held closely if at all possible. This mistaken belief can lead to intimidation, because intimidation is a way to gain more power in a situation.

Literacy coaches can effectively assist a group member who seems fearful of losing power by making visible the power that that person does have. For instance, coaches can demonstrate that they are listening to that person and that that person's ideas are being considered by the group. More explicitly, literacy coaches can ask intimidators to play a role in the discussion, such as note taker or facilitator, or to share examples of their successes as teachers. Often, with just a little attention, a person who is feeling an urge to intimidate will start to feel that they do have power in the group, and the intimidation urge will fade.

Literacy coaches can also make visible their limited power. For instance, literacy coaches can use language that indicates it is up to participants to decide what to do. I frequently "invite" group members to look at a handout, suggest they try something "if they care to," or check in to see if the activity is meeting their needs. In these ways, I show that I am there to help, not to boss. In addition, I try to openly admit what I don't know and frequently ask others to help me learn about their perspectives. These are additional ways that group members can recognize that I am a learner and as fallible as anyone else, which can make potential intimidators less fearful.

The structure of group meetings can add to or lessen group members' fear. For instance, if literacy coaches make clear that the professional learning team's activities will be steered by the members' concerns and interests, not by the literacy coaches' wishes, potential intimidators will be less fearful that the group is going to rob them of control. Or, when an atmosphere of comfortable trust is created, group members may be less likely to worry that their mistakes will be "caught" and pointed out in an embarrassing manner. Anything a literacy coach does to create a productive, participant-oriented, and comfortable group climate can help to defuse an intimidation event.

Sometimes, though, intimidation isn't nipped in the bud. Often because it takes literacy coaches and other group members by surprise, intimidation is allowed to continue for an indefinite amount of time. By the time a literacy coach collects his or her thoughts and begins to think about how to respond, it is too late. At that point, the intimidator may fear that a change in his or her behavior would be perceived as "backing down," which would be a sign of the very powerlessness about which the intimidator is so concerned.

If intimidation has gone on in a group for more than one meeting, or if the literacy coach's (or other group members') attempts to diminish conditions that cause fear or feelings of powerlessness have failed, then the only recourse is to talk to the intimidator. Literacy coaches who attempt such a conversation may find that it backfires, but it is probably worth the effort. I encourage coaches to talk to intimidators outside of group meetings, in the intimidator's classroom if possible (on "home turf," the intimidator will feel more comfortable), and to use their best communication strategies. Say "I" more than "you," demonstrate body language that shows openness and comfort, and enter the conversation with as much centeredness as you can muster. Begin the conversation by saying something like this:

> I've noticed when the team meets that some members are not saying much, and I'm wondering if you can help me with that. I sense that they feel intimidated by your knowledge. Would it be possible for us to strategize how we could help those participants feel comfortable speaking up?

A statement such as this acknowledges the contribution that the intimidator makes to the group—in this case, knowledge—and asks for the intimidator's help. Such remarks may be easier for the other person to receive graciously, because they may make the intimidator feel less powerless or anxious. Of course, comments about what the intimidating person contributes positively to the group should be sincere; mention only attributes that you truly see as making a contribution, or potentially making a contribution.

If talking to the intimidator fails to produce changes in the learning team's functioning, it may be best to disband the team and work with its members individually or in pairs. Literacy coaches may want to do this slowly, so it doesn't seem like they are panicking or like the team has failed. On the other hand, the team shouldn't have to meet time and time again when serious intimidation is taking place. One additional meeting is probably enough. I always encourage literacy coaches to be honest—in the long run, dishonesty catches up with a person and leads to mistrust—so I would resist the temptation to make up an excuse for suggesting that the group disband. Rather, a literacy coach might say,

> In our last two meetings, it seemed that we weren't very productive. Sometimes when this happens, a group needs to reconsider its purpose and how its members work together. The purpose of this learning group was, well, learning, in a supportive environment. I think maybe that we'd accomplish that better if we worked in pairs rather than as a team. What do you think?

A concept some psychologists talk about is "the elephant in the living room." This term refers to a problem about which everyone in a group is aware but of which no one speaks. In the case of a professional learning team with an intimidator, such an elephant is usually present. Everyone knows that an intimidator is attempting to increase feelings of power or control, and yet no one wants to talk about it. In suggesting that group members reconfigure their team, I attempt to neither point directly to the elephant ("Susan is intimidating Mary and Roy") nor to pretend it isn't there by being dishonest ("Could we meet individually because I don't have this time slot open any longer?"). Rather, I acknowledge that the group is struggling and that it may be better to work in a different configuration.

Intimidation is one of the greatest challenges in serving as a literacy coach. When addressing intimidation, literacy coaches are wise to be as prepared, reflective, and centered as possible. In addition, they will be assisted by a stance that assumes that all people are basically good despite the human flaws we all possess.

Sample Coaching Session: Addressing Intimidation

> *Coach:* When we met last time, we agreed that at this meeting we'd talk about ways to make the parents of our English language learners more comfortable with our literacy program and think about how they can support their kids at home. But first, I'd like to ask how it's going?

Pearl: I'm still really worried about Rosa *[a student]*. I know she knows more English than she is showing in reading workshop, but I think she's confused about which language to use when.

Corliss: That is so colonizing! You are totally failing to understand these students' multiliteracies and to recognize the code switching that they are doing in multiple sites across their lived experiences!

(pause)

Coach: Corliss, I think there are some complex ideas in what you've just said. Can you say more.

Corliss: (sigh) If we would do some reading of the literature of sociolinguists and semioticians, it would all be clear.

Coach: I think reading some shared material could be great. What do the rest of you think?

(silence)

Coach: I'm not sure what this silence means! *(self-conscious chuckle)*

Pearl: Um, I think I'm mainly worried about helping Rosa right now.

Coach: Say some more, please.

Pearl: I might have time to read some of the things Corliss is talking about over the summer, but right now I just have to help my kids.

Corliss: But that anti-intellectual stance is what gets us in trouble in the first place!

(silence)

Coach: Don, what are your thoughts.

Don: Well . . . I'm pretty worried about the five kids in my classroom who aren't reading or writing any English.

Coach: Tell us more, please.

Don: I need some ideas fast about how to help them.

Coach: Do you think reading some of the material Corliss has referred to would be a useful next step?

Don: Um . . . I'm not sure.

Coach: What about you, Monique?

Monique: I know, Corliss, that you've read all this stuff, and that's great. But I'm just trying to get through my first year of teaching and trying to get these kids to pass the state test. Maybe in the summer, like Pearl said . . .

Corliss: (sigh)

Coach: Let me see if I'm hearing all of you accurately. I think I hear that Pearl, Don, and Monique are looking for some practical answers to problems they are facing right now. I think I hear Pearl and Monique say they might be interested in reading some of the things Corliss is referring to, but not until summer. I hear Corliss saying that she knows some concepts that have helped her to frame these issues, and she wishes we all knew them, too. Am I hearing you all correctly?

(pause)

Pearl: I think so.

(Don and Monique nod their heads.)

Corliss: Yeah, I think so, too.

Coach: So would it make sense for us to develop a plan something like this. Let's aim for some practical steps to take right now and to discuss in May whether we might take on a reading project now. Meanwhile, Corliss, given that some of us have limited time, is there a way you could help us understand one of the theories you talk about, in a way that we could translate it into practical ideas for classrooms right now?

Corliss: Hmm . . . it's pretty hard to sum up. And some of this is not about practice, it's about thinking!

Coach: I know there's a concept called praxis, and I think it's the idea that a person can sort of go back-and-forth between theory and practice. Does that apply here at all?

Corliss: Maybe. But it requires an understanding of theory as well as a focus on practice.

Coach: I hear you. You are telling us that we need theory in order to make good decisions about practice, I think. Do I have that right?

Corliss: Yes.

Coach: And I hear the others in the group not feeling that they have time for that, despite your encouragement. Could you help us with the theory part, maybe by explaining a bit of it as it relates to practice?

Corliss: Well, I'd have to think about that and do a little preparation.

Coach: (smiling) Do I hear a "Yes" there?

Corliss: OK.

Coach: Meanwhile, Pearl, Don, and Monique, what next steps would you like to take?

Monique: I need practical ideas for getting the kids ready for the test.

Pearl: And like we said at the last meeting, we need to get these kids' parents involved – now.

Coach: I hear concern for time in what you say. You sound like you are in a hurry.

Pearl: Yes!

Coach: My wish is that we could do this work in a manner that allows us to be reflective and careful. Can that happen right now?

Pearl: Good point. We don't just want to jump onto some bandwagon.

Monique: No offense, but the state test is coming up in two months.

Coach: So, is it fair to say we want to do good, careful work but also feel the pressure of testing?

Monique: Yeah, exactly.

Coach: So how do we proceed?

Pearl: Well, could we look at a little research, and listen to Corliss's theories, but also develop some steps to take to help the kids? I don't think it has to be either–or.

Don: I support Pearl. Let's move ahead, but let's not be knee-jerk about it.

Coach: How do we help Monique with her concern about testing?

Pearl: Monique, you're not going to be fired in your first year because of test scores. I know you're feeling a lot of pressure, but you can only do so much.

Monique: I hear you, Pearl. But I want the kids to do a good job on the tests.

Pearl: We all do. But we are only human. Let's do what we can between now and March.

Coach: I think I hear a plan starting to develop. But before we get to a plan, could I ask what result you are hoping for with a plan? How will our work here make a difference for the students . . . ?

16 Facilitating Book Study Groups

Overview

What

- Lead a professional learning team in reading, discussing, and reflecting upon a piece of professional literature.

Why

- A study group expands the information a professional learning team has at its disposal. Through their discussion, members of a book study group engage in a kind of sociocultural/sociolinguistic learning process that expands the participants' repertoire of discourses.

How

- Participants select a book of mutual interest, read it, and discuss it.

To Think about in Advance

- How can group members feel ownership in selecting the book and participating in the discussion?
- How can this study group help participants stretch their thinking and beliefs?

To Think about During

- Is the conversation "real" or more the kind of conversation that is done for the sake of pleasing the leader or pretending to be involved?

To Think about After

- Do participants in the study group want to follow up in individual conferences about any aspect of the discussion that needs clarification or that they are trying to apply to their classrooms?
- Are members of this group reaching a point where they may want to share their new knowledge and insights with others?

Black-Line Masters Included in This Section

- **Comparing Our Group and the Author Chart.** Use this chart to help group members consider how they want to respond to differences they find between themselves and the author of a professional book.

Discussion

In some contexts, all teacher professional learning teams are referred to as study groups. However, I prefer to distinguish a specific kind of study group, the book study group, from other professional learning team activities and, to avoid confusion, I avoid calling other learning teams study groups.

Book study groups form when groups of teachers decide to read the same professional book and discuss it together. In addition to providing opportunities to increase knowledge, such groups can lead to shared discourse, connectedness, a sense of professionalism, changed instructional practices, and the development of mutual questions (Birchak et al., 1998; Sweeney, 2003).

Despite the fact that book study groups have become quite popular among educators, they still don't always go smoothly. Among the struggles are: engaging in genuine conversation; addressing differences that participants have with the author; managing the time required to read during our busy professional and personal days, and transferring new insights and learning to practice. I'll provide suggestions for literacy coaches in each of these areas. Of course, because book study groups have most of the characteristics of other group coaching meetings, suggestions from other chapters in this section also apply to book study groups.

Engaging in Genuine Conversation

In regard to the kinds of conversations that are possible in book study groups, the range is similar to that in book conversations we foster among our students. Some groups talk about a book in only superficial ways or perhaps only to feel that they have "done the assignment." Other groups engage in rich conversation and reflection that challenges participants' thinking productively and leaves everyone with a sense of renewal and growth. The difference is certainly in the nature of the conversation and the structure of the group, but also in the reasons that participants have for being a part of a group.

In order for conversation to be genuine in a book study group, participation must be genuine. In other words, participants need to choose to be there and to make that choice because they see value in reading, reflecting, and discussing. If participants join a book study group only to receive professional development credits or because they feel required to participate, they will likely engage in a superficial way. Therefore, savvy literacy coaches facilitate the development of book study groups in a manner that ensures that each member chooses to be there for the purpose of professional growth. Strategies that help ensure this fact include:

- Describe the purpose of the study group and the content of the book to be read in detail before participants decide whether to join it, so they are well informed when making that decision.

- Offer book study groups only as a voluntary activity.

- Help potential participants identify a book that is complex enough to yield interesting conversation. Typically, such a book provides more than just teaching suggestions. Seek books that offer a mix of theory, research, reflection, and practical ideas, if at all possible.

- At the book study group's first meeting, invite participants to talk about why they chose to be a part of the group. This will help group members think about their purpose for being there.

- Ask book study group members to try to stay with the group for the duration of its meetings, but tell them as well that, if they find they are no longer benefiting from the group, you'd like them to visit with you. In that way, you can learn how to facilitate the group differently to accommodate participants' needs.

- Invite participants from each book study group to share a little bit about what the group learned with the rest of the school staff, at the termination of the group's work. This will help future potential book study group members know what to expect.

Regarding the conversation that takes place in a book study group, literacy coaches can easily apply what they know about facilitating genuine conversation among PK–12 students in book discussion groups. For instance: ask open-ended questions that require more than a literal reading of the book; seek to "step into the shadows" of the conversation as soon as you can see that the participants are engaging each other to avoid making your questions or ideas the focal point of the conversation; engage participants in start-up activities as needed to get the conversation going, such as "Save the Last Word for Me" or "Sketch to Stretch" (Short & Harste, 1996). When using such start-up activities with adults, though, explain the activity and ask whether they'd like to use it to get the conversation rolling, rather than merely telling them to do it.

If you find that you are doing a lot of the talking or that you continue to be asking questions to steer the conversation even after the group has been together for a while, share this insight with participants and ask their help in thinking about what to do. One of the delightful aspects of facilitating group work among teachers is that they often have a great deal of experience in facilitating such work themselves. Therefore, when a problem is presented to them in a neutral, non-judging way, they usually have ideas about what to do. For instance, in the case of the literacy coach taking too prominent a role in leading the discussion, the group may decide to rotate leadership of the discussion, to do a little individual writing to collect their thoughts before the discussion begins, or to use additional start-up strategies to get themselves going.

Addressing Difference with the Book's Author

Occasionally a book study group will become bogged down by one or more participants' focus on how the book's author is representing teaching situations that are so different from participants' that the book can't be useful to them. For instance, I've heard teachers express concern when reading Nancie Atwell's work that the small-town nature of her students' lives prevents the work from being relevant to educators in urban areas. When such differences become a focal point for discussion, it may be helpful to talk about which differences with an author are significant and which aren't. In addition, it may be helpful to discuss differences that are significant but that participants would like to overcome by learning from the author's insights and experiences. For instance, when reading *On Solid Ground* by Sharon Taberski (2000), some teachers note that Taberski works in a literacy-focused school and wonder if they can accomplish the same things as she without having a principal and colleagues who share their commitment to such a vision. I've found it helpful to think about which differences between Taberski's school and other teachers' schools can be overcome by doing something similar or compensating in some way, and which differences have to be acknowledged as indeed significant.

Discussions about the nature of differences between authors' teaching lives and the experiences of book study group participants can be a useful strategy for literacy coaches who want teachers to see that there is typically value in learning from a wide range of educators, regardless of how much alike the reader and author are. In addition, some book study group members' concerns about such differences are motivated by a desire to reject ideas that they find too challenging. In breaking down the differences and looking at each one, the author's ideas may not seem as intimidating to those group members. Finally, some differences *are* important, and a discussion about them can help study-group participants deepen their understandings of the variety of ways that teaching, learning, and literacy are constructed by various authors as well as themselves.

Managing Time to Read

Teachers often struggle to find the time to read professional literature, and this dilemma is certainly familiar to literacy coaches as well. In my experience, the only really good solution to this dilemma is to find the time to do the reading. However, there are some sort-of-good solutions that help as well:

- Spend half of the book-study-group meeting time reading and half discussing.
- Divide the chapters of the book among members and ask them to summarize their parts for the rest of the group. Usually, this works best if all group members still read the opening and closing chapters and if those who are facilitating the discussion of any particular chapter offer suggestions about sections of that chapter which they recommended reading.
- Read only a selected portion of the book.
- Commit to reading a certain amount of minutes per week and agree that wherever an individual is in the book after reading that long will be acceptable to the other group members.

Sometimes study groups decide to read articles instead of books, with the understanding that articles will demand less reading time than books. I have mixed reactions to this approach. Choosing to read a collection of carefully selected articles that provide a range of viewpoints on a topic or a deepening single perspective can be a rich experience indeed, sometimes richer than reading a book. I would support a study group making this choice. However, choosing articles only for the purpose of reducing the amount of reading time may be flawed reasoning, because articles that present rich thinking and contextualized understandings usually take as long to read as a chapter in a book. In addition, articles on a topic should be carefully selected, and a group acting only on a desire to save time may not take the necessary care in choosing. Literacy coaches might want to ask good questions to help a study group think about these matters before deciding to read articles instead of a book.

Translating New Learning and Insights into Practice

At their best, book study groups provide teachers with new insights, ideas, and perspectives. However, participation in a book study group does not always lead to changed practice. Literacy coaches can play an important part in helping teachers make this transition.

Some participants' changed practices might be teaching strategies, some might be ways of organizing for instruction, and some might be assessment practices. In all of these cases, literacy coaching processes may be of assistance. For instance, when teachers wish to try different teaching strategies, literacy coaches can assist them by creating a vision of how their classrooms and students will be different when the strategies are implemented, developing a plan for getting to that outcome, deciding how to gauge the success of their efforts, and supporting teachers as they forward the action. These processes are fairly common literacy coaching processes and are discussed in other chapters of this book.

On the other hand, for some teachers who participate in book study groups, the change they experience is in their thinking rather than their practices. These teachers may find their habits of mind have changed significantly due to their participation in the group's discussion of and reflection about the book. I encourage literacy coaches to seek ways to strengthen those habits of mind to help teachers draw upon them on a regular basis.

Literacy coaches strengthen teachers' habits of mind most by asking good questions. Such questions are open ended and put responsibility for reflection on the teacher. These questions might include: How do you know? What do you think? On what do you base that claim? What will that look like and sound like? How will your students be different? What are your students doing? In addition, these questions may refer directly to the book just read. For instance, a literacy coach may ask a teacher, "Given what we've been talking about in the book study group, is your perspective on this matter any different?" Or "What do you think [the author of the book we just read] would say in response to this situation?" These questions remind teachers of the new learning they have just done.

Literacy coaches may want to reconvene book study groups at three- and six-month intervals to revisit ideas and perspectives from the book. These follow-up meetings help participants continue their reflection and their attempts to translate new learning into practice. In addition, they support the concept of professional growth as a journey rather than an event.

Book study groups can be extremely valuable in making a difference for teachers and schools. However, effective facilitation of those groups on the part of literacy coaches can make a difference in their success.

COMPARING OUR GROUP AND THE AUTHOR

Book:

Author:

Study Group Membrs:

Characteristic of Author	Different but the Difference Doesn't Matter	Different but the Difference Can Be Overcome	Different but the Difference Can't Be Overcome

17 Facilitating Extended Inquiry

Overview

What

- Support professional learning teams as they ask big questions about teaching, learning, and literacy.

Why

- Extended inquiry enables teachers to reflect and learn together in response to significant issues.

How

- Facilitate team members' asking questions, collaborating to seek answers, engaging in reflection and data analysis, and refining their practices and perspectives.

To Think about in Advance

- Do all members of the expanded inquiry group understand the nature of the work ahead?
- How can participants find time for expanded inquiry?
- What structures and processes will help this group be successful?

To Think about During

- Is the inquiry that is taking place authentic, in that it is driven by participants' questions and reflections?
- What additional resources will help this group find solutions and broaden their perspectives?

To Think about After

- What difference are the new learning and insight from the extended inquiry making in day-to-day classroom experiences for teachers and students?

Black-Line Masters Included in This Section

- **Data Kinds and Sources.** This form can be used to guide participants in an inquiry group to brainstorm possible data that might be useful for the inquiry project.
- **Inquiry Plan.** Use this two-page form to develop an overall plan for the inquiry process. Add to the plan at each meeting.

Discussion

A great deal of information is available on teacher inquiry and teacher action research (for instance, see Cochran-Smith & Lytle, 1992; Hubbard & Power, 2003). When teachers engage in the processes of extended inquiry, they investigate their own questions by gathering information; analyzing what they've learned; setting goals; trying new approaches to what they do and how they think about teaching, learning, and literacy; evaluating the success or impact of their efforts; and continuing to take these steps recursively until they move on to new issues or interests. In other words, the processes of extended inquiry are very much like the processes used by literacy coaches during individual and small-group meetings. What distinguishes extended inquiry is the "extended" part.

Extended inquiry is bigger than other problem solving or investigations in up to three ways: the number of people involved, the length of time involved, or the size of the inquiry. Typically, extended inquiry is done by a professional learning team that includes several teachers or even an entire school staff. The significance is not in the number, per se, but in the fact that a critical mass of teachers in one school is engaged in inquiry together. As well, extended inquiry takes a significant period of time. Again, there is nothing important about the amount of time in and of itself, but it is significant because the time involved reflects the commitment and depth of the work. All of this indicates that the inquiry involves an examination of a question or issue of significance. For instance, whereas an individual teacher may inquire into why students in her classroom are not applying knowledge of word families studied in spelling class to their writing assignments in science, a professional learning team consisting of all a school's teachers in the fourth, fifth, and sixth grades might engage in extended inquiry to understand how they might make their overall spelling program more effective.

Literacy coaches who are adept at the processes for individual and small-group coaching will have a head start in facilitating extended inquiry. However, there are a few additional skills and strategies that will assist literacy coaches with this role.

Making Teachers Aware of Extended Inquiry as an Option

Most teachers have heard of inquiry or teacher action research but don't think of it as something they would engage in. I find that a good way to introduce the possibility is to mention it as an option when brainstorming about how to address a significant problem. I "toss out" the idea as one of several and don't pursue it heavily. However, by mentioning extended inquiry as an option, I've brought to teachers' attention the possibility that it is something in which they might engage.

It also helps to have some examples of extended inquiry available. Journals such as *Language Arts*, *Voices from the Middle*, and *The Journal of Adolescent and Adult Literacy* regularly provide articles that exemplify this work done among teachers. There are many books that also demonstrate extended inquiry; I like *Spelling Inquiry* by Kelly Chandler and the Mapleton Teacher-Research Group (1999). This very readable book gives a useful description of the manner in which an entire school staff explored questions related to their spelling program, including the steps they took at each stage of their year-long extended inquiry. In addition to detailing this group's processes of extended inquiry, the book provides some interesting insights about spelling instruction.

Developing a Great Question

Coaching teachers to develop a great question for extended inquiry begins, like all other coaching, with listening and learning. Use strategies for gathering information to learn about teachers' interests and situations—and to help them gain further insight into these matters themselves. Ask about the outcome that is sought and inquire what that will be like for the students, the teachers, and their classrooms. Then, as in goal setting, periodically ask teachers to attempt an inquiry question.

Qualities of a strong question for inquiry are characterized in Figure 17.1. In general, a strong inquiry question is one which is significant, is worth the time and effort, is focused enough to be clear about what is being inquired into, and has a complex answer rather than a one-word response.

Collecting an Array of Data

Teachers new to the inquiry process usually need help in understanding the term "data," particularly in understanding that the term refers to a range of information, both qualitative and quantitative, which informs the inquiry process. It may be useful to provide an example of an inquiry project which used a broad range of data from many sources, in order to give participants a "real life" example. Assist teachers in brainstorming all the kinds of information they might seek and all the sources which might provide it. Figure 17.2 lists sources of possible data.

Analyzing Data

Data analysis is a process that is partially logical and partially intuitive. At the root, it is about making sense of a complex array of information. If some or all participants in an inquiry group are unfamiliar with data analysis, the literacy coach will want to take leadership in this process. However, all participants should be included in data analysis, both to encourage their learning as well as to benefit from their insights. When all members of a group contribute to making sense of data, the analysis is enriched.

A danger in analyzing data, particularly when attempting to answer a complex question, is trying to fit all data into a single tidy category. A related danger is paying attention only to those data that fit into

---

Qualities of Strong Questions for Inquiry

- The question is significant to all members of the inquiry group.
  - Weak: How can students read math problems more successfully? (When some members of the inquiry group don't teach math.)
  - Strong: How can students read directions in assignments and on tests more successfully?
- The question is "big" enough to merit the time and effort involved in the inquiry.
  - Weak: What effect does teaching "fix-up strategies" have on students' independent reading?
  - Strong: Which strategy instruction supports student success in independent reading?
- The question is focused enough so everyone has the same understanding of what is being asked.
  - Weak: What are some effective ways to begin the school year?
  - Strong: What processes are effective in preparing students for successful participation in writers' workshop?
- The question's answer is complex—it can't be answered with a single word or phrase.
  - Weak: Does a mandatory study skills class help high school students?
  - Strong: How can the study skills of high school students be strengthened?

Figure 17.1. Qualities of strong questions for inquiry.

such a category. For instance, if teachers in an inquiry group are seeking ways to teach poetry more effectively, they may be tempted to look for a practice that is *the* best way to teach poetry. In doing so, they may ignore a great deal of data that contradict their single-practice answer. A more effective way to analyze data is to look at all of the information they provide and to be willing to attend to the complex picture they paint of the subject at hand.

Consider the possibilities when a group of people attempt to order a pizza. If the group members try to find one pizza topping they all like, they may end up with a pizza that is not representative of the taste of any of them. On the other hand, if they recognize the range of tastes in the group, they may order two pizzas with different toppings on each half. In this way, they get a more complex order that satisfies all their needs. In analyzing data, the goal is not to find the one "topping" that

---

Sources of Possible Data

Interviews with:
- Parents
- Students
- Teachers
- Researchers
- Community members
- Alumni

Statistical data from:
- Student assessments
- Attendance information

State/district profiles

Analysis of documents such as:
- Report cards
- Meeting minutes
- Annual reports
- Professional development handouts/agendas
- Student literacy activities
- Lesson plans
- Curricula
- Web sites

Student behavior such as:
- In-process reading
- In-process writing
- Literature discussion groups
- Book selection
- Editing
- Computer use

Self-observation of:
- Teaching
- Learning
- Reflecting
- Literacies

Observation of:
- Students
- Teachers
- Others engaged in literate acts
- Musicians, artists, dancers

Professional literature

Transcripts of:
- Teaching episodes
- Student interactions

Figure 17.2. Sources of possible data.

fits all the data but rather to see the complex picture that all the data present.

Among the strategies that might be used for data analysis are:

- Sorting data—putting like with like and then seeking to create categories by labeling each of the groups of similar data
- Statistical analysis—seeking to draw conclusions about data based upon analyses of the likelihood that one factor influences another
- Numerical analysis—counting occurrences, responses, or some other quantifiable information
- Representing data in picture or chart form and looking for patterns or impressions
- Sharing data with others who are not in the inquiry group and getting their impressions and insights
- Writing about the data and sharing the pieces of writing among inquiry group members
- Learning how similar data have been analyzed by others, typically by reading about others' research, and doing the same with the data at hand.

Data analysis requires a certain amount of time. In fact, with a complex set of data, it could go on almost infinitely. I encourage inquiry groups to set aside three to five meetings for data analysis, in order to provide an adequate amount of time both to analyze data and to think about the data between meetings. At some point, though, participants in data analysis need to decide that it is time to move on. One way to make this decision is to watch for redundancy: when the same insights or conclusions are being drawn repeatedly, the data may be adequately mined.

Trying and Revisiting

After data analysis, participants in inquiry are usually thinking practically—the "so what?" of the project is on their minds. It is time to try some new things in their classrooms. An important tool at this stage is a gauge for whether their efforts are effective. If the inquiry group spent a great deal of time envisioning the desired outcome of the project at the start, they may have a strong sense of what success will look like. However, savvy literacy coaches will encourage group members to think about how they will gauge their success by helping participants identify signs of success, tools they can use to collect information about possible success, and criteria for determining success. This is similar to the process used on the Planning for Action Chart during individual or small-group coaching.

As participants try new teaching strategies, new ways of interacting with students, new class or curricular arrangements, or make any other changes prompted by the inquiry, they will likely want to revisit the data collected in the inquiry process. In doing so, they can fine-tune their efforts. For instance, if a group of teachers is seeking more effective ways to engage English Language Learners in their classrooms, and as a result of their inquiry they try using more visuals, they may find that they are not seeing the signs of success they had hoped for. At that point, they may revisit the data and decide that perhaps the data indicate that students who are English language learners are more engaged when they themselves are producing and using the visuals. Therefore, the teachers in the inquiry group will tweak their use of visuals.

Sharing Results

I encourage inquiry groups to share their efforts and their results with others. When inquiry projects are shared with others in the same school building, they serve as inspirations for similar work and they keep colleagues informed of new efforts toward more effective teaching and learning. When inquiry projects are shared outside the school building, at district-level meetings, at professional conferences, in local newspapers, and in professional journals, they contribute to the professional knowledge base, they indicate the efforts of teachers to continually learn and grow, and they demonstrate the effectiveness of inquiry as action research. In an era when the demand for "research-based" practices is high, it is especially important that effective research done by teachers for teachers is given the attention it deserves.

Sample Coaching Session: Inquiry Groups

> *Coach:* At our last meeting, we prioritized concerns and developed a topic for inquiry. The topic we agreed upon was student reading outside of school. We agreed that at this meeting we'd develop an inquiry question and a plan for collecting data. Could you start out by telling me more about the topic?

> *Olive:* I think by fifth grade, the kids are losing interest in reading outside of school. They have so many interests and activities, and then they just like to veg out and watch TV or play video games.

> *Tyrell:* And the boys especially aren't motivated to read. They don't think it's cool.

> *Coach:* What else can you tell me?

Debbie: I think the kids still like to read when they do it in school. They just have better things to do—at least, in their opinion—outside of school.

(pause)

Coach: What do the kids tell you?

Debbie: They say they are too busy to read.

Tyrell: The other day, I was showing the kids some science fiction books, because they are all excited about movies like the *Star Wars* movies, and I offered to let them take some of my own science fiction books home. One of the boys, Robert, said "Man, why would we read the books when we can rent the movies and play the video games?" I think that he spoke for most of the boys, and some of the girls, too.

Coach: Do you think this is more of a problem for the boys than the girls?

Debbie: I think so, to an extent, but not entirely.

Coach: What percent of your female students choose to read outside of school for pleasure?

Olive: I'd say 50 percent.

Debbie: I agree.

Tyrell: Yup.

Coach: And the male students?

Olive: Twenty percent.

Tyrell: No, about 5 percent.

(pause)

Coach: Debbie?

Debbie: Oh, I don't know. Let's say 10 percent.

Coach: I hear that students of both genders are not reading as much as we'd like, but it is more of a problem with males. Do I have that right?

Various Participants: Yup. Yes. OK.

Coach: What have you tried?

Tyrell: I demonstrate all the time that I'm a reader, and I talk to them about books I think they'd be interested in.

Debbie: I assigned independent reading for homework for years, but I finally gave up because it was a losing battle.

Olive: Me, too. Mostly, I give book talks and encouragement, and, like Tyrell, I make sure the kids know I love to read. Oh, and I talked to parents at Open House about the importance of reading at home.

Coach: You've tried several things: demonstrating your own interest in reading, assigning reading as homework, encouraging interest in particular books, and speaking with parents. Anything else?

Olive: One year, we made individual charts with reading goals on them. It helped a little, but it was just too much work.

Coach: I hear that another attempt you made was to have students chart their individual reading goals, but it was too much work.

Olive: Right.

(pause)

Coach: What would it look like if this problem were solved?

Olive: All of the kids would read!

Coach: How much?

Tyrell: I don't expect the kids to read every night. I know they're busy. But if they read a couple of nights a week, maybe two hours' total, that'd be great.

Debbie: I could live with two hours.

Olive: That would be wonderful.

Coach: Would that be your goal—to have the students read outside of school for two hours every week?

Various Participants: Yes. I agree.

Coach: Then, what question do you have about this goal?

Tyrell: How do we get there?

Coach: Can you describe "there?"

Tyrell: How do we get all kids to read two hours per week outside of school?

Coach: Let's consider that as an inquiry question. Is it workable?

Debbie: I like it. It says exactly what we are aiming for.

Olive: But maybe it's too specific. I mean, there's not going to be research that specifies exactly two hours per week.

Tyrell: What about, "How do we get all kids to read outside of school?"

Olive: That's better.

Coach: Is it a question you think you can answer after you have done some investigation?

Olive: I don't know. I'm not sure that I know how to get all kids to do anything. And if anyone did, they'd be rich!

Tyrell: But it's what we want to do.

Olive: Yes, but can we answer the question for sure?

Tyrell: Well, we can make some attempts. We can try some things; we can try to influence the kids.

Coach: So I hear you saying, Tyrell, that you want to influence the kids to read?

Tyrell: That's probably all we can do.

Coach: Would this be a more realistic question: "How can we influence all kids to read outside of school?"

Olive: That's definitely doable.

Tyrell: I like it.

Coach: When you have answered it, will you have information that will help?

Olive: I hope so. It should.

Tyrell: If I knew how to influence all the kids, I'd be very pleased.

Coach: What does this question mean to you?

(pause)

Olive: What do you mean?

Coach: Well, I want to make sure that you all are trying to answer the same question. I want to make sure we all agree on what the question means.

Olive: Oh, well to me it means that we want to know how to persuade kids, how to use our influence, to get them to read.

Tyrell: It means that we can't guarantee every student will read, but we want to maximize the chances by using all of our powers of persuasion and our ability to make an impression on the kids.

Debbie: I think it is a question about us—about what our influence really is—but in order to answer it, we have to learn more about the kids.

(pause)

Coach: Anything else?

(silence)

Coach: Does the question seem to mean the same to each of you?

Participants: Yes. Yeah.

Coach: Here is a chart that describes a good research question. Do you think this one meets the characteristics? *(Coach distributes copies of Figure 17.1.)*

(pause)

Debbie: I like this—the question should be big enough. This question feels that way.

Olive: Can you repeat the question?

Coach: Sure. Here's what I wrote down: How can we influence all students to read outside of school?

Tyrell: Yup. It has these characteristics.

Olive: I agree.

Coach: Debbie?

Debbie: Yes. I think it is good.

Coach: OK, we have a question for inquiry: "How can we influence all students to read outside of school?" I've written that on the Inquiry Planning Sheet. Now what kind of information will help you answer that question?

Debbie: I want to know why kids do read, what motivates them.

Coach: OK, do you mind if I record these on the chart paper?

All: Great.

Tyrell: And why don't they read?

Debbie: That's good. How about, "What influences kids to read?"

Tyrell: And when do they see others reading, especially role models, like athletes.

Coach: Hold on a minute. I'm trying to keep up.

(pause)

Coach: OK, what else?

Olive: I'd like to know what parents think about reading at home, and whether they encourage it.

Debbie: And do kids even have books at home?

Tyrell: Do kids have library cards?

Debbie: Do they use our school library?

Tyrell: Do they buy books or get books for presents?

Olive: What kind of things would the kids read if they did read?

Debbie: Do the kids understand the importance of reading outside of school?

Olive: Do we understand it?

Coach: Say some more, Olive.

Olive: Well, why do we encourage it?

Tyrell: And do the other teachers in the school encourage it?

Olive: I'd like to know how much time the kids spend in organized sports and music lessons.

Tyrell: And how much time they play video games and watch TV.

(pause)

Debbie: Do you think there is some research on this that we could find?

Coach: Now you are thinking about some sources of this information. That's the next column on my chart. Let's go back and forth between the two columns . . .

DATA KINDS AND SOURCES

Use the left-hand column to brainstorm information that might help in answering the inquiry question. Use the middle column to brainstorm sources that might provide that information. Then, after discussion, place a check mark in the right-hand column to indicate the data that will be collected.

Information	Source	✓

INQUIRY PLAN

Inquiry group members:

Inquiry question:

Why is this question significant?

Data to be collected:

Data	Source	Who is responsible?

Major insights as a result of the data analysis:

Plan for changed practices, arrangements, or interactions as a result of the inquiry:

Evaluating Progress

Success Looks Like/ Sounds Like	Tool(s) for Collecting Data	Indicator That Goal Has Been Met

Timeline:
    Data collection completed by:
    Data analysis completed by:
    Initial implementation and evaluation completed by:
    Follow-up and revisiting of data completed by:
    Share results with others by:

Section 4: Processes for Demonstration Lessons

Some literacy coaches see demonstration lessons as a cornerstone to their practice, while others see such lessons as tangential to coaching conversations with individuals and teams. This section will place demonstration lessons in perspective and provide suggestions for making them effective parts of coaching processes. Co-teaching, a more complex form of teaching occasionally done by some literacy coaches, will also be addressed.

18 Effective Demonstration Lessons

Overview

What

- Demonstration lessons are connected to the overall coaching process by helping teachers to further their goals related to greater student success.

Why

- When demonstration lessons are connected to teachers' goals, they are meaningful and are responsive to teachers' needs.

How

- Embed demonstration lessons in the coaching process by providing them as they grow out of coaching conversations and by connecting them afterward to further conversations and actions.

To Think about in Advance

- Is the purpose of this demonstration lesson clear to me and the teachers involved?
- Have teachers indicated that this demonstration lesson will help them meet a goal?
- How can I fit this lesson into the curriculum, activities, and interests of the students in the teacher's classroom?
- Would I like the teacher(s) to do something specific during the lesson?

To Think about After

- What points do I want to make about my work when I meet with the teacher to debrief?
- Have I reflected adequately in order to prepare for the debriefing?
- What questions will help the teachers to connect this lesson to the goals we have established?

Black-Line Masters Included in This Section

- **Demonstration Lesson-Planning Sheet.** This form provides spaces for planning all aspects of the demonstration lesson and for writing reflective notes afterward.
- **Teacher Observation Sheet.** This form may provide some questions for teachers to consider as they watch a demonstration lesson.

Discussion

Literacy coaches usually recognize demonstration lessons as one of their duties. In fact, some literacy coaches place demonstration lessons at the forefront of their work, seeing demonstrations as the place to start. This is a mistake, because when coaches start with demonstrations, they usually start with whatever is on their minds. Rather, literacy coaches need to get to know teachers and learn about their interests and concerns, and then provide demonstration lessons as appropriate, in order to further teachers' work toward their goals.

The literacy theorist and author Frank Smith has helped me to think more carefully about demonstration lessons. In an e-mail message he wrote to a colleague, he makes a distinction between demonstration lessons and model lessons. Smith says,

> A demonstration always makes engagement possible, the learner can identify with what the demonstrator does. Modeling, on the other hand, is merely a matter of showing how something is done. It is not something the teacher is personally interested in at the time, and it is not something that the learner can engage with. Engagement (identification) does not take place; nor, generally, does learning. (personal communication, 2005)

Smith's ideas suggest to me that the phrase "demonstration lesson" is different than "model lesson" in an important way. A demonstration lesson is an example; it's not necessarily the only one, but it's a useful one. On the other hand, a model lesson is one that is presented as the preferred or "model" way to teach. In other words, a model lesson is provided as the exemplar, as *the* way to approach a problem, whereas a demonstration lesson is provided as an option, as a possibility. For Smith, a demonstration lesson leaves the conversation open and supports teachers as decision makers whereas a model lesson tells teachers what to do. This distinction could be described as the difference between "best practices," which would be modeled, and "possible practices," which would be demonstrated. Such a distinction might also ease the concerns of literacy coaches that they have to provide a "perfect" lesson as they demonstrate.

If a demonstration lesson is one of an array of potential practices, how do literacy coaches decide which demonstration lessons to do? When the lessons are embedded in coaching conversations, the decision is much easier: demonstration lessons further teachers' movement toward their goals. In most instances, several demonstration lessons might be possible, but during the coaching conversation, the coach and teacher decide which one seems useful at that time.

For example, let's say that a teacher has a goal of helping students to predict more often when they read. The literacy coach might suggest several teaching strategies that support students' predictions, and the teacher may note that she is unfamiliar with one of them, the Directed Reading-Thinking Activity (DR-TA) (Allen, 2004). Out of this coaching conversation, then, comes a need for a demonstration lesson, because the coach and teacher agree that the teacher will understand DR-TA better if it is demonstrated as well as discussed with the coach.

Literacy coaches sometimes ask me how they can know all the possible demonstration lessons they might suggest in response to a teacher's goal. I remind them that it isn't necessary to be the expert in any situation. Rather, literacy coaches can provide some options and can also turn to other sources for possible options. Teachers themselves usually have some ideas, too, about how they might solve a problem or what demonstrations they would like. In other words, literacy coaches are not the sole source of ideas but rather one source, and effective literacy coaches find sources more often than they are *the* source.

When literacy coaches do provide demonstration lessons, they are wise to prepare by discussing two matters with teachers:

- What role will the classroom teacher play? Some teachers prefer to sit in the back and watch, but others prefer to take notes, interact with students, or co-teach part of the lesson. Occasionally, literacy coaches find that teachers fail to stay in the classroom during demonstration lessons. If this is a problem, I suggest providing teachers with an observation sheet or asking teachers to give feedback on a particular aspect of what you are doing. Such tasks usually keep them in the classroom. Merely asking the question, "What would you like to do while I'm providing the demonstration lesson?" will prompt teachers to reflect upon their role and the importance of staying in the classroom.

- What are the students' current interests, activities, and curricular engagements? It is valuable for literacy coaches to fit their demonstration lessons into classroom routines and current curricular engagements whenever possible. In this way, the demonstration lesson is less of a disruption for the students and will therefore go more smoothly and be more productive for purposes of learning as well as demonstration.

At the start of the demonstration lesson, explain your purpose to the students, and at the end of the lesson, ask them for feedback. I find that students are interested in the activities of teachers to improve instruction and are usually excited to be part of the process. For instance, I work with a school in southwestern Indiana where the children have discussed the changes to their literacy program extensively with their teachers. They have developed metacognitive awareness of the changes in their learning and literacies, and they were pleased when the school board asked them to share their insights with them at a meeting last spring. In fact, one group of fourth-graders was excited when a teacher involved in overhauling the school's literacy program was (by coincidence of timing) appointed principal by the school board on the same evening that they shared their growth with the board. These students believe they "got the principal her job!"

Demonstration lessons are just one way that teachers can be assisted in working toward a goal. Teachers often pursue their own learning and action research by reading about a topic or issue, gathering data about it, talking and perhaps observing colleagues, reflecting upon possible action, trying some things, fine-tuning their actions, and/or repeating one or more of these steps. In addition, literacy coaches can provide many other types of support, as suggested by the other sections of this book.

Sample Coaching Session: Arranging a Demonstration Lesson

Coach: OK, your goal is to teach "second tier" vocabulary [Beck, McKeown, & Kucan, 2002] more effectively in your biology lessons. When you think about that goal, what steps do you think of taking to meet that goal? For right now, let's not worry about sequencing or evaluating them, let's just brainstorm.

Teacher: Well, I guess I could continue to highlight new vocabulary on the study sheet for each chapter. But I need some strategies for teaching that vocabulary.

Coach: Yeah, if the terms are second tier, the students aren't likely to learn them on their own.

Teacher: Right. But how do I help them?

Coach: What do you think?

Teacher: Well, I know that students need to connect new learning to what they already know, so I guess I want to help them do that. Maybe using a concept map would help.

Coach: Great. Have you used concept maps before?

Teacher: Yes, I have.

Coach: How did they work?

Teacher: Well, pretty well, but I don't think that's the only approach I should take. I feel like I need a menu of vocabulary instructional strategies. Help!

Coach: I have a few ideas off the top of my head, and perhaps we could find some more in some resources.

Teacher: OK.

Coach: Some strategies I have used that have helped include concept ladders, semantic feature analysis, exclusion brainstorming, and words sorts.

Teacher: I've heard of some of those, but I'm not sure what they are.

Coach: I can give you some handouts that explain them, and several are pretty easy. Words sorts can be done several ways, though. I would be happy to demonstrate some options for them in your classroom.

Teacher: That would be great.

Coach: Do you see a chapter or unit coming up that has some heavy-duty vocabulary?

Teacher: The unit on cells is full of vocabulary. I'd love to have you demonstrate word sorts during that.

Coach: OK, glad to do so. Let's look at the calendar . . .

DEMONSTRATION-LESSON PLANNING SHEET

Teacher(s) goal:

Date of demonstration lesson:

Location of demonstration lesson:

Objectives of lesson:

Background information:

    Students:

    Curriculum:

    Class rituals/rules:

Role of classroom teacher during lesson:

Post-lesson reflections:

Date and time for follow-up discussion with teacher(s):

TEACHER OBSERVATION SHEET
(for use by *the teacher* during demonstration lessons)

1. What strategies do you see being demonstrated? What details do you notice about how the strategy is being implemented (for instance, what is the coach saying or doing)?

2. What signs of student success do you notice? What conditions are facilitating this success?

3. What signs of student frustration do you notice? What conditions are contributing to this frustration?

4. What adaptations would you make to this lesson?

The Literacy Coach's Desk Reference: Processes and Perspectives for Effective Coaching by Cathy A. Toll © 2006 National Council of Teachers of English.

19 Demonstration Lesson Follow-up

Overview

What

- Reflect upon the demonstration lesson and plan for continued work toward the goal in coaching conversations after the demonstration lesson.

Why

- Demonstration lessons are effective when they are embedded in the entire coaching process, emphasize thinking as well as behavior, and help teachers apply the content of the demonstration in working toward their goals.

How

- Share reflections and ask key questions to help teachers think about the demonstration and plan to try demonstrated practices themselves.

To Think about in Advance

- What are my own reflections on the lesson that I demonstrated?
- How can I use the follow-up conversation to advance teacher thinking?

To Think about During

- Does the conversation promote teaching as a thinking, problem-solving practice?
- Is it clear to the teacher that this was a demonstration lesson, not a model lesson?

To Think about After

- What other support can I provide as the teacher or teachers continue to work toward this goal?

Black-Line Masters Included in this Section

- **Post-Demonstration Follow-up Conversation.** This form assists literacy coaches in planning for follow-up conversations and in facilitating them.

Discussion

Providing a demonstration lesson without a follow-up conversation is like building a house with only half a roof: it isn't very effective, because the job hasn't been completed. When literacy coaches do this, they send the message that the importance of the demonstration lesson is in the coach's behavior. In other words, they imply that observing behaviors leads to improved teaching and, thus, that teaching is about behavior. I'd suggest that teaching is more about thinking, problem solving, and relationships, and therefore the meaty part of a demonstration lesson is the reflection and conversation that take place before, during, and after.

When I plan a demonstration lesson with teachers, I establish the date and time of a follow-up conversation at the same time. Then, when I have completed a demonstration lesson, I jot my own reflections in preparation for that conversation. In this way, I ensure that the follow-up will indeed take place and that I am ready for it.

The purposes of a follow-up conversation might be any of the following:

- Listen and learn from the teacher regarding which aspects of the lesson appeared to help students and which aspects might be modified.

- Share your own reflections upon the lesson: What was successful? What do you wish you would have done differently?

- Discuss the decisions you made during the lesson and the reasons for making them.

- Answer questions, both those asked by the teacher of the coach and those asked by the coach of the teacher, for the purpose of reflection and clarification.

- Provide an opportunity for the teacher to think about how the demonstration lesson may influence his or her own classroom practices.

- Plan modifications that the teacher is going to make to the strategies and practices that were demonstrated.

Note that only the final two items on the list above refer to the teacher's adoption of new practices as a consequence of the demonstration lesson. Sometimes, follow-up conversations focus only on these matters, but I prefer a different approach. If the entire point of a follow-up conversation is to say, in effect, "So, how are you going to change your practices to be more like mine?" the implicit messages are that the coach is the expert, that there is one practice that is best, and that the purpose of coaching is to change behaviors. I disagree with all of these notions.

As with all literacy coaching, the coach's first task in a follow-up conversation is to listen and learn, and asking good questions can facilitate that process. Some questions I find useful are in Figure 19.1.

Literacy coaches may find it difficult to be candid with teachers about the lesson they taught, much less to listen to teachers' reflections, which may refer to aspects of the lesson that didn't go as well as the coach wished. Because we are human, many of us struggle to have our limitations made visible to others. However, the openness with which a literacy coach reflects upon the lesson has the potential to be an effective part of the follow-up conversation. Because effective teaching includes problem finding and problem solving, and because effective teaching is *not* about having no problems, literacy coaches demonstrate key habits of mind when they discuss what they'd do differently, how the lesson did and didn't further the students' learning, and how the lesson might be modified for greater effectiveness.

I encourage literacy coaches to avoid thinking or behaving like some real estate agents who act interested in the "customer" only to the extent that it makes the other person think they have a bond and therefore influences the customer to buy whatever the agent is selling. Rather, maintain the collaborative professional conversation you've been having all along and, when it comes time to learn teachers' responses to your demonstrations, maintain a goal of supporting teachers' reflection, not

---

Questions for Follow-up Conversations

- What surprised you about the demonstration lesson?
- Was there anything about which you wanted to ask me?
- May I share some of my decision making during the lesson?
- What did you notice about the students during the lesson?
- Are there modifications to the lesson that might be useful?
- Does this lesson help you in working toward your goal?
- When you think about what it will look like and sound like when you meet your goal, did you see any of those characteristics during the lesson?
- What else could you try?

Figure 19.1. Questions for follow-up conversations.

supporting your ego or the assumed value of any particular teaching practice. A metaphor that is more appropriate for this stance than the real estate agent is the personal trainer who observes what the newly-fit client is able to do, wants to do, and feels comfortable trying next. Interestingly, personal trainers are occasionally called . . . coaches!

The demonstration lesson follow-up conversations will usually fold into conversations that support planning for action. In other words, beyond discussing the demonstration lesson itself, literacy coaches and teachers usually focus on the next steps for meeting a goal. Occasionally, instead of moving ahead toward the goal, coaches and teachers find themselves revisiting the goal. For instance, a teacher who observed her students struggling with social studies vocabulary even when the literacy coach was using great vocabulary-learning strategies may have the insight that her students' struggles would best be solved not by teaching more strategies but by helping the students read to answer their own questions rather than reading to complete the assignment. Thus, a new goal and new plan of action are created.

When the follow-up conversation is consistent with other effective coaching conversations, it will be important and meaningful regardless of what conclusions are drawn. Literacy coaches are well-served if they maintain a stance that coaching is about reflection, mutual professional collaboration, and problem solving, but above all about helping teachers identify their strengths, grow those strengths, and develop new strengths.

Sample Coaching Session: Demonstration Lesson Follow-up Conversation

> *Coach:* Thanks for meeting with me. As you know, I want to follow up with you after doing a demonstration lesson in your classroom. I've written some notes about the lesson, and I'd like to hear your thoughts about it as well. Then perhaps we can think ahead about where you'd like to go from here. First, though, I'd like to ask for your thoughts about the demonstration.

> *Teacher:* It was great. I really enjoyed watching you teach.

> *Coach:* Thanks. What did you notice that surprised you?

> *Teacher:* Hmm . . . I guess I was surprised by how engaged the students were. You really had them thinking.

> *Coach:* It's amazing how the DR-TA provokes that in readers.

> *Teacher:* Yeah, I hardly ever hear from Jorge and Mica, and they were really contributing.

Coach: Why do you think that is?

Teacher: Well . . . they really wanted to get their point across. It's like they cared that the others heard what they thought.

Coach: Can you say some more?

Teacher: Well, they had ideas that they were eager to share. They were thinking about the story they read, they had opinions about what happened and what was going to happen next, and they were excited about sharing.

Coach: I noticed, too, that they seemed to be listening to what the others had to say. One thing I listen for when doing a DR-TA is whether the students are just answering my questions or whether they are responding to each other. And I noticed that Mica in particular was paying attention to his classmates. He wanted to argue his point, but he also listened as others argued theirs.

Teacher: Yes.

Coach: What else did you notice?

Teacher: I noticed that when you asked the kids to read, they all did!

Coach: What do you think that's about?

Teacher: At first, I thought they were just being polite, because you were a guest, but after a while, I could tell they really wanted to read. Parts of that story were pretty challenging for some of them, but they all tackled it.

Coach: Why do you think they did that?

Teacher: Again, they really wanted to read. The questions you asked, the predicting . . . it made them curious. Plus, it was a good story.

Coach: I agree. Something else I noted was a sort of competitiveness to make an accurate prediction. Adolescents are so aware of what the others are doing.

Teacher: Yes, DR-TA seems perfect for middle school students because they like to engage each other.

Coach: When you think about your goal of helping students pay more attention to the meaning of what they read, do you see this demonstration as helping you?

Teacher: Absolutely. The students really understood the story, and they also went beyond literal understanding. They were interpreting the author's message and thinking about the characters.

Coach: Can you think of any modifications you would make if you implemented this strategy?

Teacher: I was wondering . . . would it work for students to write their answers instead of talking about them?

Coach: What makes you think of that?

Teacher: Well, I was thinking about the kids doing this at home for an assignment. I want them to predict all the time.

Coach: I hear you. You want the kids to be predicting like this when they read alone at home. Here's what I find: It's often the interaction with the others that motivates them to pay such close attention and to do the predicting. So for me, in my teaching, DR-TA has been most powerful as a whole-group or small-group activity in class. Think about what we've been saying about your class: For some of the students, the interactions with their classmates and the opportunity to check each other's predictions were what kept them engaged.

Teacher: I suppose so. But then how does this help them understand assignments?

Coach: In my experience, doing the DR-TA in class develops predicting as a strategy that kids apply in other situations, too. It's a habit of mind that they develop.

Teacher: Mmm hm.

Coach: A practice that encourages kids to read and think about their assignments can be to provide half the assignment the night before a discussion and then have the kids predict and read the rest in class. Or have them predict and discuss the first half in class and then read the second half the next night.

Teacher: I like that!

Coach: What else are you thinking about DR-TA?

Teacher: The story you provided was so interesting. And the kids wanted to solve the mystery. What about the other stories the kids need to read? They aren't all that good.

Coach: I hear you. Of course, students will be more engaged as readers with some materials than with others. That's true of us as readers, too, isn't it?

Teacher: Mmm hm.

Coach: I wonder if a next step would be to talk about reading selections and assignments. Perhaps we could work together to think about the purposes of assignments you make and the most useful selections for meeting those purposes.

Teacher: I like that idea. Also, could we think about what else I could do to get the kids to read their assignments?

Coach: Sure. Let's think about when we'll meet next . . .

POST-DEMONSTRATION FOLLOW-UP CONVERSATION

Participants in the Follow-Up Conversation: Date:

Topic of the Demonstration Lesson: Classroom:

Points to Make about the Decisions Made during the Lesson:

Student Behaviors and Responses:

Possible Modifications and Extensions:

Reflections upon the Usefulness of the Lesson in Helping Teacher(s) Meet Goal:

Next Steps toward Goal:

20 Co-Teaching

Overview

What

- Classroom teachers and literacy coaches co-teach to support teachers' work toward their goals.

Why

- When co-teaching, classroom teachers and literacy coaches develop collaborative relationships that further the shared reflections and promote discussion of insights and perspectives.

How

- Use questioning, information gathering, and planning for action to plan for teaching. Continue the coaching conversations after co-teaching has begun in order to discuss what is happening.

To Think about in Advance

- Will co-teaching further the effectiveness of the literacy coaching processes? Will it help this teacher build capacity?

To Think about During

- Is this a collaboration in the sense that we each contribute our strengths and respect the other's?

Discussion

I use the term *co-teaching* to describe an extensive partnership between a classroom teacher and a literacy coach. Typically, co-teaching engages the classroom teacher and the literacy coach in planning together, implementing classroom activities, and evaluating their success in meeting their objectives, over a period of days or weeks and over several engagements with the class. Clearly, co-teaching takes a great deal of time and effort, and it also requires the existence or development of a strong professional relationship.

The coaching conversations that are typical of most coaching processes, as outlined in this book, certainly continue during co-teaching. But the benefit of co-teaching is that it creates a relationship that enables much more. Co-teaching is more holistic and therefore doesn't require reliance on a single discreet goal. Rather, co-teaching supports professional learning that is complex and even more situated. The difference between co-teaching and other coaching processes is like the difference between going to a dietician for nutritional assistance and living with a spouse who, with you, chooses to overhaul eating habits. Meeting with a dietician is beneficial because it provides a supportive relationship in which the dietician listens and learns from you about your lifestyle and preferences. He or she then helps you set nutritional goals; learn new information about food, health, cooking, and exercise; and make changes. However, having a spouse who, like you, is committed to better nutrition is a totally different experience. Together you shop for groceries; plan and cook meals; provide mutual support when you "slip"; and enjoy the success of better health and well-being. This experience is embedded in daily living and provides the kind of support that only an equal partner can give.

Although many teachers of all levels of experience might enjoy a co-teaching relationship with a literacy coach, I recommend that coaches limit co-teaching to certain situations, given that it demands a great deal of the literacy coaches' limited time. Co-teaching is especially helpful in these situations:

- When a teacher has no prior classroom teaching experience and has not participated in a program of teacher education. This situation occurs increasingly in districts that hire provisionally certified teachers or teachers who are new participants in alternative certification programs. Literacy coaches tell me that such teachers lack a vision for their classroom and are often overwhelmed by teaching tasks.

- When a teacher is on a plan of assistance and must improve in broad areas in order to become effective. A word of caution: Literacy coaches should not approach teachers in such situations; that would mean that coaches possess confidential supervisory information and may even be acting in a quasi-supervisory manner. Rather, when a teacher needs to improve in significant ways, the supervisor (usually a principal, assistant principal, or department chair) should work with the teacher to develop a plan for improvement that includes literacy coaching and should then develop a plan for the teacher to approach the literacy coach for help.

- When a teacher or group of teachers is overhauling their instructional approaches or curricula and wish for a collaborator to support them through the process of making deep changes.

Table 20.1. Co-Teaching and Traditional Literacy Coaching

Co-Teaching	Traditional Literacy Coaching
Literacy coach and teacher are engaged two or more hours per day over a period of days or weeks.	Literacy coach and teacher are engaged one or two hours per week or every two weeks.
Coaching conversations focus on planning, implementation, and reflection upon overall teaching processes.	Coaching conversations focus on specific goals.
Literacy coach's role is to engage in all aspects of the teaching process, at least in a particular content area, along with the classroom teacher.	Literacy coach's role is to listen and learn, gather information, facilitate goal setting and planning for action, and forward the action.
Overall teaching success is the focus of the collaboration.	A single goal is identified and is the focus of the collaboration.
The outcome is greater student success.	The outcome is greater student success.

Table 20.1 compares co-teaching with more traditional literacy coaching. Although these differences reflect the depth of collaboration and a more holistic approach to coaching, the outcome is still student success. I encourage literacy coaches to use all of the skills they draw upon in more traditional literacy coaching, but to especially assist the teacher in determining how student success will be evident. When classroom teachers have a clear picture of what success will look like—particularly that success is far more than an increase in student test scores—they will have a guidepost to which they and the literacy coach can continually return.

In co-teaching, the literacy coach may initially take a more active role in demonstrating the reflection and decision making that goes into many kinds of teaching. Over time, though, the coach may want to take a less-active role, in a modified form of gradual release of responsibility (Sweeney, 2003). I often emphasize that in literacy coaching, teachers and coaches should remember that they are all experts in some areas and they all bring strengths to the situation. However, the purpose of co-teaching is often to help teachers gain new and sometimes basic knowledge and habits of mind, which means that the literacy coach may need to take a stronger role at the start. A wise literacy coach will still seek to understand teacher strengths and to maximize them, even if they are not from traditional teaching practices. For instance, a provisionally-certified teacher might know very little about literacy learning processes but may have a vast repertoire of stories from the oral and written traditions of her culture and the culture of many of her students. This is a strength that would merit a great deal of attention.

This example hints at a risk of co-teaching: The literacy coach may become colonizing. The term "colonizing" draws upon the practice of colonization that has been used by world powers to make another country or culture like their own in ways that eradicate what was there before the more powerful country took over (Carnoy, 1974). For instance, the colonization of what is now the United States by Europeans eradicated much of the native culture that was here and altered the quality of life of Native Americans forever. In literacy coaching, colonization might take place if a coach imposes his or her view of teaching, learning, and literacy upon the teacher to the extent that the teacher feels that the only acceptable way to behave, believe, and think is in exactly the same manner as the literacy coach. This is always a risk in literacy coaching, but especially a risk in co-teaching. The opportunities for the misuse of power are many, and some of the teachers with whom literacy coaches engage in co-teaching are particularly susceptible to colonization, because they are new to the profession or sometimes the country, in the case of the large number of provisionally-certified bilingual teachers being hired in some districts with many English language learners. In these situations as in all coaching situations, savvy literacy coaches are attuned to the workings of power and are using their best coaching strategies to promote a mutually respectful relationship.

The process of co-teaching itself is too complex to delineate in one spot. It involves all of the process of effective literacy coaching, plus all of the processes of planning for and implementing effective teaching. My advice for literacy coaches wishing to take on a co-teaching situation is that they go slowly, spend a lot of time articulating their thinking, never assuming that the other person knows what literacy coaches may take for granted about teaching, learning, and literacy, and that they still spend a lot of time listening and learning from teachers. Make visible the struggles of co-teaching, such as feeling unsure about which person will do what or determining how to proceed when the partners in co-teaching have different ideas about what to do next, and avoid an attitude of "the coach knows best."

I recommend that literacy coaches who are co-teaching remind themselves frequently of the desired outcomes and monitor to see how they are doing. In co-teaching, literacy coaches shouldn't aim to "fix" all of a teacher's problems, and a literacy coach shouldn't postpone exiting a co-teaching situation until the classroom teacher is at maximum capacity. Rather, the desired outcomes of co-teaching should aim for increasing the teacher's capacity to the point where he or she can function adequately without a co-teacher. At that point, the coaching will continue, but in a less-intense manner.

Co-teaching is a literacy coaching activity that may occur only occasionally in a literacy coach's career. Given the amount of time and attention that is required to do it well, many literacy coaches simply cannot afford to co-teach very often. On the other hand, it can be a rewarding engagement for both the literacy coach and the teacher.

Sample Coaching Session: Deciding to Co-Teach

Coach: Thanks, Maria, for meeting with me. As you know, I'm visiting with each first-grade teacher to listen and learn about their work and to see if there are ways I can support them as they support student learning. I'd like to begin by asking, when you think about the kind of readers and writers you want your students to be, the kind of teaching you want to do, and the kind of classroom you want to have, what gets in the way?

Teacher: Hmm . . . um . . . could you repeat the question?

Coach: Sure. When you think about the kind of readers and writers you want your students to be, the kind of teaching you want to do, and the kind of classroom you want to have, what gets in the way?

Teacher: I'm not sure. You know, I've never taught before.

Coach: Tell me what you've done before becoming a teacher.

Teacher: Well, I was raising my family, and we moved here to Houston from Chicago because my husband works for [an international firm]. Because my kids are older, I decided to look for a job, and my friend told me that the schools were hiring bilingual people to be trained as teachers.

Coach: When you think about being a teacher, what seems to get in the way?

Teacher: I don't know. Everything, I guess! I don't know where to begin.

Coach: Tell me about your own education, please.

Teacher: Well, I went to school in Spain; college, too. My degree is in accounting, and before I had kids, I worked for a department store, doing accounts payable.

Coach: It sounds like you are a math whiz.

Teacher: Yes, I'm good at math. But I love to read.

Coach: So do I! Who are some of your favorite authors?

Teacher: I like mysteries and suspense novels—you know, Patricia Cornwell and James Grisham, authors like that. Also, I read cookbooks like other people read novels. I love to cook.

Coach: It sounds like you have interests your students would enjoy.

Teacher: Maybe. But first I have to teach them to read and add.

Coach: I know you are working on your regular teaching certificate. What courses have you had?

Teacher: None so far. Right now, I'm enrolled in an introductory course, which starts next week.

Coach: So you're starting at the beginning when it comes to teaching. On the other hand, you have a lot to build on, having raised kids and lived in different countries, and just being an interesting person.

Teacher: I don't feel like any of that has helped me so far.

Coach: Could we work together to get you to a place where you are comfortable?

Teacher: I'd love that.

Coach: I'd like to suggest something that's a little unusual. Would you care to co-teach with me? What I mean by that is that for a couple of weeks, we'll plan lessons together. I can't be in your classroom all day, but perhaps I could meet with you every day after school, and I could be in your classroom for literacy block. Then after a couple of weeks, we'll still meet every day, but I'll only come to your classroom some days, and then we'll reduce our meetings. I'll still support you, and perhaps we'll want to work together in some way all year, but it won't be so intense.

Teacher: I'm embarrassed to have you do that much for me, but it would help so much.

Coach: No problem. It's what I'm here for. And please think of this as a partnership. We'll help each other.

Teacher: I don't think I could help you.

Coach: You are getting to know the kids well, and you speak Spanish fluently, whereas I know only a little. So we'll have to partner a great deal, and lean on one another. How does that sound.

Teacher: It sounds great. How do we begin?

Section 5: Processes for Serving the Entire School

Literacy coaches are often called upon to provide services to the entire school, such as leading professional development workshops or planning for whole-school improvement. Serving as a school leader may help literacy coaches broaden their perspective, strengthen relationships with school staff members, and share insights garnered from their coaching conversations and classroom engagements. On the other hand, serving the entire school may not enhance the first duty of literacy coaches, which is to help teachers build their capacity to help students achieve. I encourage literacy coaches to keep their aims in mind as they serve in school leadership capacities, thereby seeking connections between such leadership and coaching whenever possible and monitoring their schedules so they aren't taken away from their primary duties too often. This section provides processes for making such connections between coaching and other leadership roles and for evaluating literacy coaching in order to assess its effectiveness in meeting such aims.

21 Facilitating Non-Coaching Professional Development

Overview

What

- Provide appropriate leadership to non-coaching professional development but connect this work to coaching activities whenever possible.

Why

- Time spent facilitating non-coaching professional development is time not spent coaching.

How

- Develop non-coaching professional development activities from information garnered while coaching and refer back to these activities in future coaching conversations.

To Think about in Advance

- What topics and concerns have I heard from many of the staff members? Are there topics that can be addressed well in non-coaching professional development?

To Think about After

- What aspects of this professional development experience will be important in coaching conversations?
- Which staff members have goals that particularly link with this professional development experience?

Black-Line Masters Included in This Section

- **Teacher Interest Worksheet.** Use this form to jot topics that arise in coaching conversations and keep track of teachers who express interest in those topics. This information can assist in selecting topics for large-group professional development workshops.

Discussion

Literacy coaching is a form of professional development embedded in the daily work of educators. As such, literacy coaching is consistent with the Standards for Professional Development of the National Staff Development Council (NDSC, 2001). However, as the NDSC standards imply, literacy coaching is not the only approach to teacher professional development. In fact, Bruce Joyce and Beverly Showers, whom I call the "grandparents" of coaching in education, maintain that coaching is effective as *part* of a program of professional development that also includes workshops, demonstrations, practice, and follow-up (2002).

As schools and districts plan for non-coaching professional development activities, they are likely to turn to literacy coaches for assistance. After all, literacy coaches are typically hired because of the strength of their experience, knowledge, and skill—qualities that are sought in professional development leaders. The downside of being recognized for one's capacity to lead non-coaching professional development is that literacy coaches can find their time consumed by such concerns.

When literacy coaches tell me they are pulled too often to lead non-coaching professional development, I encourage them to have a conversation with their principal, program leader, or the entire school staff. I find that others are usually concerned when this problem is made visible, and they are usually glad to help coaches determine how much time they should spend leading non-coaching professional development and how to prioritize the work that they do in this area. For instance, if a school staff is informed that the literacy coach is available only 60 percent of the time due to demands from other duties, teachers on the staff may reflect upon other ways to complete those other duties and, as a result, non-coaching professional development duties may be shared with two or three others, including other staff members, district leaders, or faculty at local universities.

The non-coaching professional development facilitated by literacy coaches is usually in the form of large-group workshops. Such workshops may be mandatory for all staff or voluntary and are often related to school improvement plans. There are other resources available to assist literacy coaches in facilitating workshops (Garmston, 2005; Lyons & Pinnell, 2001), so I won't detail that information here. My concern at this point is that literacy coaches consider how to connect their facilitation of non-coaching professional development to their coaching conversations.

First, coaching conversations can be useful in identifying topics for professional development workshops. For instance, if a literacy coach finds that many teachers are struggling to understand miscues, he may suggest that this would be a useful topic for a workshop. I suggest to coaches that they identify topics for whole-group instruction with teachers in a manner similar to how teachers decide which topics to address in which part of a reading workshop for students. When individual students are struggling with, say, a strategy, teachers will often address that struggle in an individual conference. If a cluster of students are struggling with another strategy, teachers will often address the students' struggle in a guided reading group formed for that purpose. On the other hand, if all students in a classroom are struggling with a strategy, teachers will likely make it the focus of whole-group instruction, either in a shared reading activity or a minilesson, at least for a start. In a similar way, literacy coaches can determine which issues are best addressed with individual teachers, small groups of teachers, or the entire teaching staff. The latter issues are suitable topics for professional development workshops.

When the topics of professional development workshops are determined by a school improvement plan or a schoolwide professional development plan, literacy coaches may not have total control over the content of the workshops. However, they will likely influence those workshops, in at least two ways. First, literacy coaches can provide input into the plan when it is being developed, either by serving on the steering committee or by providing input as a member of the staff. Second, literacy coaches may be able to fine-tune the workshop topic even after it is identified. For instance, a common topic for professional development, found in many school improvement plans, is "reading comprehension." This is such a broad topic that literacy coaches can help shape it based upon their coaching conversations. For instance, coaches may recognize that many teachers are seeking ways to help students comprehend material in one of the content areas. Or, they may recognize that teachers have a good grasp of comprehension strategies but don't know how to use running records, miscue analyses, retellings, and conferences to ascertain what comprehension strategies students are using. Thus, literacy coaches can help school leaders think about what the workshop on reading comprehension might actually address.

The other important part of connecting non-coaching professional development to coaching conversations is to look for ways to make the content of professional development workshops relevant in coaching conversations. This happens after literacy coaches have facilitated the workshops, and it can take several forms:

- Referring to a point made in the workshop
- Using a copy of a handout to remind teachers of a point from the workshop
- Asking teachers whether there is anything from the workshop that will help them in meeting a goal
- Providing a demonstration lesson that includes something from the workshop

When literacy coaches make these connections between their coaching conversations and other duties, they feel that their work is more integrated and less fragmented. In addition, these literacy coaches help teachers make connections between various aspects of professional development. In this way, literacy coaches take up the advice of Joyce and Showers to create a seamless whole of professional development (2002).

TEACHER INTEREST WORKSHEET	
Topic	**Persons Interested**
	1. 2. 3. 4. 5. 6.
	1. 2. 3. 4. 5. 6.
	1. 2. 3. 4. 5. 6.
	1. 2. 3. 4. 5. 6.
	1. 2. 3. 4. 5. 6.

The Literacy Coach's Desk Reference: Processes and Perspectives for Effective Coaching by Cathy A. Toll © 2006 National Council of Teachers of English.

22 Participating in School Improvement Processes

Overview

What

- Align school improvement processes with literacy coaching.

Why

- Literacy coaches possess information about staff interests and needs that can contribute to school improvement planning.

How

- Advocate for continued collaboration and coaching conversations while supporting the development of a schoolwide vision of needed improvements.

To Think about in Advance

- How can I support teachers' participation in directing their own growth?
- Can I help the staff to broaden the kinds of data that they use in developing a school improvement plan and/or their understanding of that data?

To Think about During

- Am I advocating for the teachers I work with and not just myself?
- Do my statements reflect what I know about the teachers in this school?

To Think about After

- How can I support the school improvement plan while continuing to coach for teacher growth?

Discussion

Most schools in the United States are now required to develop an annual school improvement plan (SIP). In some ways, a SIP is parallel to a coaching conversation. Look at this list of components of school improvement plans provided by the office of the State of Washington Superintendent of Public Instruction (2005):

- Assess Readiness to Benefit
- Collect, Sort, and Select Data
- Build and Analyze the School Portfolio
- Set and Prioritize Goals
- Research and Select Best Practices
- Craft Action Plans
- Monitor Implementation of the Plan
- Evaluate Impact on Student Achievement

Just as in literacy coaching, the process of developing and implementing a SIP may involve using data, setting goals, planning for action, and forwarding the action. SIPs typically include other components as well, such as school attendance figures, information about technology use and parental involvement, and a professional development plan (Indiana Department of Public Instruction, 2005). However, at its best, a SIP results from the reflection and decision making of a collaborative group of educators and can lead to teacher growth.

I am told, however, that school improvement planning sometimes does not take place in this ideal manner. Instead, it may be done haphazardly, or in a top-down manner, or in a manner that fails to address important issues in the school. When SIPs are developed in these ways, they are often meaningless or serve as sources of frustration for teachers.

As building leaders, literacy coaches may be asked to participate in developing and/or implementing SIPs. Some literacy coaches see their involvement in SIP teams as ways to further their work and others see such involvement as an obstacle to effective coaching. The purpose of this chapter is to offer suggestions for maximizing SIP planning and implementation in a way that makes it compatible with other literacy coaching activities.

My suggestions for literacy coaches related to SIPs fall into three categories: participating in the SIP planning process, participating in the SIP implementation process, and staying on track when the SIP could easily steer you off-track.

Participating in the SIP Planning Process

Literacy coaches who participate on a leadership team responsible for the school improvement plan are wise to use their best coaching skills of listening and learning, asking good questions, and gathering information, for starters. Don't assume that the process is going to be a waste of your time or a contradiction of your purposes. Seek to understand the perspectives of all participants and honor those that differ from yours. Do your homework and understand what your state or district requires in the name of school improvement planning and what is optional. Share such information in a nonthreatening, collaborative manner.

An important role literacy coaches can play in school improvement planning is to help the team think about the variety of data that might be considered in developing the plan. SIP requirements universally mandate that student achievement test scores must be included, but many states and districts allow for additional data as well. Even if your SIP requirements are strict about including no additional data, you can still invite the team to consider such data in its discussions and conversations. Data that can be useful in considering a school's status in literacy learning and achievement are provided in Figure 22.1.

Literacy coaches can also influence the way literacy learning and teaching are conceptualized by the SIP team. Is literacy considered as only its parts—that is, an accumulation of subskills—or as something more than its parts? Are only reading stories and writing expository information considered valuable, or are multiple texts considered? Is the term *literacy* restricted to meaning reading and writing or does it include speaking and listening? Would the team be ready to think of literacy even more broadly, such as the way sociolinguist James Gee (1999) uses it to indicate the ability to use a discourse powerfully in a particular situation? Is teaching perceived as a top-down process, an interactive process, or an apprenticeship-styled process?

Similarly, literacy coaches can influence the manner in which professional development is thought about in SIP planning. Literacy coaches who value coaching processes of the kind described in this book will want to encourage their SIP teams to consider similar processes. For instance, the professional development plan in the SIP will be most effective if it supports teachers as reflective decision makers rather than implementers of programs or behaviors. Better yet, the SIP plan will support collaborative teaming and inquiry to maximize its impact on the school culture. Of course, the role of the literacy coach will be evident in this plan, with job-embedded professional development taking precedence over whole-

Survey results from:
    Students
    Parents
    Teachers
    Community leaders
In-process reading data
    Miscue analyses
    Running-record data
    Informal Reading Inventory data
In-process writing data
    Focused observation notes
    Samples of successive
        drafts
Library information
    Books checked out
    Voluntary usage
    Holdings—changes over
        time
Technology information
Multiple literacies
    Technology literacy
    Art, music, dance
    Sign systems in science/
        math
Oral language usage
    Tape recordings

Observation data
    Periodic focused
        observations
    Checklist observations
Report card data
Student products
    Writing samples
    Journals/logs
    Project evaluations
Self-assessments
    Student
    Teacher
Interview data
    Burke Reading Interview
    Interest inventories
    Parent interviews
Classroom environment
    inventories
Technology usage data
Concepts of print
Integrated unit projects
Critical literacy projects
Media literacy projects

Figure 22.1. Literacy-related data that might be included in planning for school improvement.

group professional development, which may be evident but will not be the only or most important form of support for teacher growth.

Participating in the SIP Implementation Process

Literacy coaches occasionally panic when they recognize that their work is part of a school improvement process, as it often is, and therefore they must "show results." After all, it takes time to develop relationships and support teachers in setting goals, planning for action, and forwarding the action. A literacy coach who begins this work in September may not feel she has accomplished even the first steps with all teachers until December or later. When achievement tests are given in March, as they are in many schools, and when achievement test scores are considered the major indicator of success, as they are all too frequently, literacy coaches and their colleagues may become concerned. They may have a strong sense that literacy coaching is important in their school, but they may fear that the achievement test scores will fail to demonstrate this importance.

It is true that literacy coaching takes time, and it may seem like a slow process to some. However, there is no productive way to rush it. When literacy coaches hurry, they often stop listening and learning and start telling and prescribing. This shift increases teacher resistance but not coaching effectiveness. Savvy literacy coaches honor the amount of time it takes to do coaching work and then collect additional data to show that they are having an impact. This data will likely be of the sort described in Figure 22.1 earlier in this chapter, as well as program evaluation data of the kind described in Chapter 23.

In addition, savvy literacy coaches will remind teachers, parents, and others repeatedly of the purpose for literacy coaching. Literacy coaching supports and develops strengths, and therefore it increases the capacity of a school's staff to teach effectively and respond to the range of challenges that arise in every educational setting. It might help to use a metaphor. Literacy coaching is more like creating a strong retirement account rather than earning a large salary. In other words, it is an investment that bears fruit over time. If it is done carefully, it will probably yield great benefits but not so much in the present as in the future. It will optimize teachers' capacity over time in ways that will make them wealthy with insight and reflective habits of mind as well as strengthened skills. It is important for literacy coaches and other school leaders to remind themselves and others often that literacy coaching is a capacity-building act.

Another concern literacy coaches sometimes have with SIPs is that they feel pressure to address a particular SIP goal in their coaching conversations. For instance, if a school staff includes in its school improvement plan a goal to improve the vocabulary learning in science and social studies of all students, the SIP team may then expect that literacy coaching will focus on this goal. I encourage literacy coaches to work with the SIP team to help them understand that coaching must respond to the goals of individual teachers and teams of teachers as well as the goals of the entire staff. One way to do both—achieving an "and" solution rather than an "or" solution—is to take the SIP goals to coaching conferences and to share them with teachers when reviewing the purpose of the meeting, in a modified form of The Question. It might sound like this:

> Thanks for meeting with me. As you know, I'm meeting once again this year with all teachers to talk about their work and their plans for the year, and to listen and learn about how I might be of support as you work to help your students achieve. We have SIP goals that include vocabulary instruction in science and social studies, and as a geography teacher, that goal may influence your think-

ing. However, I'd like to begin by asking, as you think about the understanding you want your students to have about geography, and you think about the kind of teaching you want to do, and you consider the kind of classroom you want to have, what's getting in the way?

Staying on Track When the SIP Interferes

Because this is not an ideal world, literacy coaches sometimes find that their efforts are not in sync with a school improvement plan. This tends to occur in the early years of a school's involvement in literacy coaching, when the coach is not as involved in SIP leadership and/or when coaching processes are not yet a part of the school culture. In these instances, the SIP may contradict a literacy coach's efforts, either by emphasizing a different approach to literacy or a competing approach to professional development. For instance, a SIP may emphasize phonics instruction in isolation while a literacy coach is helping teachers help their students use their phonics knowledge in reading meaningful text. Or a SIP may emphasize whole-group professional development workshops and ignore coaching processes.

I advise literacy coaches in these situations to continue to do their good work despite the SIP. If they are developing strong relationships with teachers and engaging in ongoing coaching conversations, their efforts will no doubt supersede the effects of the SIP. I discourage literacy coaches from openly working against the SIP, in the sense that they fail to participate in plan-dictated workshops or denigrate the plan as without worth. On the other hand, I encourage literacy coaches to ask good questions and, when appropriate, explain the rationale for their work and their thinking. Literacy coaches who are not already part of the SIP team should join it, and if they are a part, they should take leadership in helping SIP team members to think more broadly about what the plan could include and how it could be consistent with the literacy coach's efforts. Chances are that the members of the SIP team are stuck in one way of thinking about SIP details and professional development planning, and literacy coaches can, over the course of some months, help them see that there can be more value added to the plan when the content is shifted.

On occasion, literacy coaches may find that the contradictions between the SIP and their intentions and work are not from a lack of insight or awareness but reflect a significant divergence of views. In these situations, wise coaches remember that their first job is to listen and learn. In doing so, they will develop an understanding of why others on the SIP team have different perspectives and how significant these differences are to the coaches' ability to do their work. In the case of a school that conceptualizes literacy and professional development in ways opposite to the coach, literacy coaches will need to have patience, take the long view, and work diligently to ask questions, share information tentatively when others may be ready for it, document the effects of their work, and repeat it all over and over again. They may also find it helpful to engage in conversations about beliefs and values related to literacy, learning, and teaching, because they and the other staff will likely find shared beliefs and values that will give them a foundation upon which to build additional shared concepts and practices Perhaps some literacy coaches will choose instead to take another job. I can't fault them for this; sometimes we need to move to find a better fit for ourselves and those with whom we work, and a coach need not feel bad if this is his or her choice. After all, a frustrated literacy coach can become an angry literacy coach who then will lose effectiveness. On the other hand, if literacy coaches can find some sources of support and can sustain their efforts over time, they will no doubt make a difference.

Sample Coaching Session: Talking to the SIP Team about Competing Perspectives

Andrea: OK, then, we have decided that one of our goals will be to increase students' fluency in reading. What can we do for professional development?

Tad: I heard a speaker at the state convention who had some great tricks for teaching kids to read with expression. I think she's at the university. Could we bring her in?

Rebecca: Oh I know who you mean! Dr. Jones. She's great—really funny, and with lots of practical ideas. She could do a workshop in September.

Tad: Yeah, that's who it was. I agree; let's have her do a workshop.

Andrea: Sounds good. And maybe she could do another one later in the year. Maybe in January on our professional half-day?

Coach: I'm glad we have a goal related to fluency. I notice that some students think their reading task is to "sound good" rather than to understand. It will be important to help teachers recognize that fluency instruction at its best will help kids read more successfully.

(pause)

Tad: Well, that's what Dr. Jones does, right?

Coach: I haven't participated in any of her workshops. But I wonder if we can ask her to help us connect meaning construction to fluency.

Andrea: You mean, when kids are reading with expression, they should also be comprehending?

Coach: Maybe. But I think fluency is about more than reading with expression. And sometimes I see kids worrying about "sounding good" rather than understanding.

Rebecca: I know what you mean. Sometimes they are worrying about what paragraph they'll read when it's their turn to read aloud, so they aren't paying attention to what the story is about.

Tad: Oh, I get it. You want us to make sure the kids keep paying attention to the story and not when it will be their turn to read.

Coach: Well, that could help. But I think it's bigger than that. I think fluency is about using the information you have as a reader in an integrated way to make a prediction, check the prediction, and fix it up if needed, in a way that helps you keep reading and understanding.

(pause)

Andrea: I'm not sure I get it.

Coach: Yeah, it's more complex than it seems on the surface. Hmmm . . . could I bring an example to our next meeting? I could show how you as readers can be fluent or not, and how it would affect your comprehension.

Andrea: Well . . . we only have a month to get this plan developed.

Marty: I'd like to hear what she has to say. I think this is interesting.

Andrea: I agree it's interesting. But does it make a difference to our SIP?

Coach: I see. We could continue developing the plan, due to time shortage, but then we could think about fluency a bit before Dr. Jones comes in.

Andrea: That would work. Can we say we'll have a workshop in September and January, and then you can explain this to us when we meet next week?

Coach: Sure. And I promise to take no more than fifteen minutes. But here's another thought . . . could we also include my work in the professional development plan?

(pause)

Tad: What do you mean?

Coach: Well, coaching is job-embedded professional development. So my work can become another way to support teacher growth in fluency instruction.

Tad: You mean you'll give each person information on fluency when you coach them?

Coach: Well, you know me. I like to let the teacher set a meaningful goal. But I could remind teachers of the SIP goals and ask if any of those goals influence the teachers' goals.

Andrea: Thanks. That would be great. OK, I'm writing down that we have three professional development activities for this goal . . .

23 Evaluating Effectiveness of Coaching

Overview

What

- Provide leadership to the evaluation of the effectiveness of the literacy coaching program.

Why

- Literacy coaching can always be improved, and evaluation can help direct that improvement.

How

- Use a variety of assessment tools and practices and involve as many people as possible.

To Think about in Advance

- What are my goals as a coach, and how can I assess my success in meeting them?
- What resources will help in developing an evaluation?
- Who should participate in the evaluation process?
- How can this evaluation be ongoing?

To Think about After

- With whom should I share the findings of this evaluation process?
- How can the evaluation be even more effective the next time around?

Black-Line Masters Included in This Section

- **Literacy Coaching Evaluation Plan.** Use this form to develop an overview of the evaluation process. Ask the evaluation team to assist in creating the plan.

Discussion

Evaluating our effectiveness has become rather standard in education for everyone, including literacy coaches. I encourage literacy coaches to meet with their supervisors to discuss what evaluation is planned and to volunteer to do more. Most literacy coaches are classified as teachers and are evaluated in the same way that teachers in their school are evaluated. While this process may be useful, it will not provide as much information as a more detailed and complex evaluation process. You don't want to offend your supervisor by implying that her or his evaluation is inadequate, so I'd encourage you to use language similar to this:

> I look forward to your evaluation of my work. I'm wondering . . . could we also evaluate the literacy coaching program overall? I would be glad to do the grunt work if you will support me and provide direction.

The purpose of a deeper evaluation of the literacy coaching program is to provide information about how well the program is meeting its goals and how well it is meeting appropriate standards. If you don't have goals for your coaching program, develop some now, with the assistance and feedback of your supervisor and the teachers with whom you work. Then, plan for evaluation.

Standards for literacy coaching can be found or developed from several sources. The International Reading Association (IRA) has developed standards for middle school and secondary literacy coaches in collaboration with the National Council of Teachers of English, the National Council of Teachers of Mathematics, the National Council for the Social Studies, and the National Science Teachers' Association (go to www.reading.org.) In addition, IRA has developed a position statement about reading specialists that includes information about literacy coaching, and its standards for the preparation of reading specialists include literacy coaching. When I worked at the North Central Regional Educational Laboratory (NCREL), I developed an article on selecting Reading First literacy coaches that includes information about the qualities such coaches should have (2004). As well, refer to your own job description for an idea of the target for which you aim.

In addition to considering the characteristics, skills, and strategies that you want to display as a literacy coach, though, think about the goals and characteristics that your literacy coaching program should have. You may want to review paperwork that was developed to conceptualize the program, be it a grant application, proposal for a school board, or SIP. Get input from teachers early and often about what they want the literacy coaching program to be like and work with them to craft ongoing and annual goals for the program.

Among the tools you might use for evaluating the effectiveness of your program and your literacy coaching, consider the following:

- Interviews of teachers, students, administrators, parents, and other staff members
- Evaluation surveys completed by teachers, students, administrators, parents, and other staff members
- Analyses of documents such as coaching notes, newsletter messages, demonstration lesson plans, reflective journals, and work logs
- Videotapes of coaching conferences or demonstration lessons
- Self-assessments

Invite others to assist you in analyzing the data. Because this is a time-consuming task, you don't want to ask too many people or wear anyone out. You might think about gathering a small team of two teachers, your principal or other supervisor, and another literacy coach from another school. After data are collected and analyzed, develop some initial evaluative statements and ask a larger group—perhaps the entire school staff—to provide feedback. Then craft the statements into final form.

Use the evaluation statements to develop a three-part plan: What will stay the same, what will you change, and what will you continue to think about or evaluate. With this plan, you will demonstrate that you are taking the evaluation to heart and that it is an ongoing process. Share the statements and plan with all staff members, parents, and others in the school community.

LITERACY COACHING EVALUATION PLAN

Date:

People on the Evaluation Team:

Goals of the Coaching Program:
1.

2.

3.

4.

Standards to Be Used in Evaluating Work of the Literacy Coach:

Evaluation Tools to Be Used:

Tool	Deadline for Administration/Collection	Person Responsible

Deadline for Data Analysis:

Deadline for Development of Plan:

Findings and Plan Will Be Distributed to:

The Literacy Coach's Desk Reference: Processes and Perspectives for Effective Coaching by Cathy A. Toll
© 2006 National Council of Teachers of English.

Section 6: Processes for Serving Individual Students

Before schools had literacy coaches, they had reading specialists. As a result, some educators confuse the roles of these individuals, especially because, in some cases, the same people who served as reading specialists are now serving as literacy coaches. In general, reading specialists have a number of clients whom they serve, including students, parents, administrators, and teachers. On the other hand, literacy coaches have one client group: teachers. Despite this fact, literacy coaches are often asked to work with students. I stress that when literacy coaches do so, they are not coaching. Nonetheless, they often do work with students, either to help out, to avoid hassles, or because they are asked to divide their time between serving as a literacy coach and serving as a reading teacher. This section provides suggestions for connecting literacy coaching to work done with students when working with them in small groups or when evaluating them.

24 Connecting Small-Group Instruction and Coaching Activities

Overview

What

- If working with small groups of students is one of your assigned duties, connect it to literacy coaching whenever possible.

Why

- Your work with small groups of students provides concrete experiences that can facilitate coaching conversations with the students' teachers.

How

- Demonstrate your reflective thinking in planning for instruction; listen and learn from the teacher in a manner that prompts the teacher to be increasingly reflective; work with the teacher to be an informed instructional decision maker regarding the students with whom both of you work.

To Think about in Advance

- What have I learned in providing small-group instruction that will be of use to the classroom teacher?
- What does the classroom teacher know that will be useful to me in providing small-group instruction?
- How can I bring my work with the students into the work of my coaching conversations in a way that will help the teacher build capacity?

To Think about During

- Am I serving as a resource but avoiding the trap of acting like the expert in regard to these students?

To Think about After

- Have questions arisen about students in the small group in response to which I might collect data?

- Has the classroom teacher given me new "lenses" through which to perceive the students?
- During the coaching conversation, was there a balance of sharing between both myself and the teacher?

Discussion

Many educators who serve as literacy coaches part of the time are asked to serve as instructors of small groups of students at other times. They may be serving a Title I pull-out program, acting as Reading Recovery teachers, or working on a regular basis with guided reading groups. At these times, these educators aren't serving as literacy coaches because their clients are students, not teachers. However, savvy literacy coaches will find ways to bridge their work with regularly assigned small groups of students to their work as literacy coaches. (Note: In writing this chapter, I'm not advocating for splitting a literacy coach's duties like this. I understand that such splits are caused by complex factors—including budgetary limitations, staff limitations, and program requirements—and it is outside the scope of this chapter to debate the pros and cons of such an arrangement. What I do know, however, is that these splits occur frequently in the lives of literacy coaches.)

Several connections can be made between literacy coaching and working with small groups. Among them are:

- Discussing with the students' classroom teachers the decisions you have made and vice versa
- Sharing assessment data you have with classroom teachers and vice versa
- Using the students in your small group as examples for topics being discussed in the coaching conversation
- Inviting classroom teachers to watch you while instructing students in a small group, and asking to watch teachers while they instruct the students in the classroom setting. Share insights. (Perhaps a third teacher can help by "covering" for a classroom teacher, who can then reciprocate for that teacher at another time.)
- Assisting classroom teachers in reflecting on progress toward their goals by sharing insights that you have about the students in your small group
- Co-conferencing with students along with their classroom teachers
- Trying new practices or assessments with a small group of students that teachers are trying as well and then comparing notes and refining practices together

When discussing students with their classroom teachers, literacy coaches run the risk of being didactic in the manner by which they share information. Such one-sided information-providing can be avoided if literacy coaches strive to establish true coaching relationships rather than what I call a "telling relationships." When literacy coaches work collaboratively with teachers, they approach conversations as opportunities to listen and learn, share, reflect together, and plan thoughtfully.

For instance, in the past as a reading specialist, I would meet periodically with teachers to tell them what I knew about the students and how I was helping the students become more successful. I answered teachers' questions, and I asked what the teachers saw in their own classrooms, but I was there more as the expert than as a collaborator and coach. On the other hand, as a coach, I now meet with teachers to listen and learn as well as tell. The teachers and I share what we know about the students, using a variety of data, and together we ponder how we can use this information to plan for instruction.

When literacy coaches engage in conversations with those teachers whose students the coaches also teach, the coaches have an opportunity to demonstrate reflective decision making and problem solving. In other words, when you are wearing your "teacher hat," you have the opportunity to practice, refine, and share your habits of mind. Then, in meeting with the students' teachers, you can create a mutuality in which you and the classroom teacher are engaged in similar processes together, rather than always finding yourself in the position of leading the teacher to be the reflector and problem solver.

Sample Coaching Session: Connecting Coaching and Small-Group Instruction

> *Coach:* Last time when we met, we agreed to work together on helping the students be more fluent in using a wide variety of cues smoothly and interactively. We agreed to do a mini-case study by looking carefully at two students: Mandy, who I know from Title I, and Curtis. But first, I'd like to ask you how it's going?
>
> *Teacher:* Well, I've been taking lot of notes about Curtis and Mandy. I think I know them better as readers, especially based on the miscues I've gathered from the running records.
>
> *Coach:* Tell me more, please.
>
> *Teacher:* Well, I see that Mandy is hesitant to take risks. She wants to be absolutely sure of a word before she reads it, and in the process she often loses track of what she's reading.

Coach: Can you give me an example?

Teacher: Sure. Look here. When the text said, "Paolo couldn't imagine why his parents were so angry when he got home," Mandy stopped when she came to "why." I know she has read this word a million times, but I don't think she was expecting it in the flow of the sentence. So she just stopped cold.

Coach: I see. I bet with that sentence structure, she was expecting the word after imagine to be the name of something Paulo couldn't imagine.

Teacher: Yeah, that's what I think, too.

Coach: What did she do?

Teacher: She just sat there. I prompted by asking what would make sense, and she just stared at the paper. I asked her to say "blank" and read to the end of the sentence, but she seemed so thrown that that strategy didn't help her. Eventually, I just told her.

Coach: I see some of that when she reads with me, too. Look here; she stopped cold twice when she was reading in a conference with me yesterday. But then look here; she didn't seem familiar with the word *superstitious*, but she made several attempts. She didn't get it, but she tried.

Teacher: I see. Does that happen very often?

Coach: Let me look. Well, in the running record before that, she never stopped cold. She tried every time she came to something she didn't know. She made one productive substitution and two guesses that were phonetically pretty good even though they didn't make sense.

Teacher: Hmmm.

Coach: Let's look more carefully at these miscues from all three passages and see if we can get any more insight . . .

25 Addressing Needs for Student Evaluations

Overview

What

- Provide your expertise in assessment of literacy without doing every special evaluation. Connect assessment work to coaching whenever possible.

Why

- You know a lot about literacy assessment and don't want to appear selfish about keeping it to yourself. On the other hand, you have a limited amount of time and could spend a lot of it doing student assessments.

How

- Create resources for student evaluation and help teachers and others use them. Connect assessment work with literacy coaching by using student evaluation data for decision making and problem solving.

To Think about in Advance

- How much support does this teacher need in order to evaluate the student successfully?

To Think about After

- Have I supported the teacher adequately?
- Which assessments seemed easiest and which seemed most difficult? Do I need to provide more assistance with the latter?
- What insights about the child being evaluated have been drawn and can they be useful to the coaching conversation?

Black-Line Masters Included in This Section

- **Cover Sheet for Assessment Packet.** Include this form at the front of a packet of assessments that you gather together to help classroom teachers in doing student evaluations. Provide directions in writing as well.

Discussion

Literacy coaches are often the most knowledgeable people in a school when it comes to assessing student literacies. Therefore, when a student is particularly puzzling or is being evaluated for special services, literacy coaches may be called upon to do an evaluation. If they refuse to provide such assistance, they look selfish. If they agree, however, they may spend a lot of time on evaluations. In addition, whenever literacy coaches do something that others could learn, they are failing to build the capacities of those other educators.

An effective approach to this dilemma is to do everything for teachers *except* the actual evaluation. Meet with the teacher first to listen and learn about the child and the purposes for the evaluation. Then pull together a set of assessments and place them in a binder along with instructions. Review the items in the binder as needed, and arrange a time to meet with the teacher and answer further questions after the teacher has had a time to look them over. After the evaluation, meet with the teacher to review the data collected and to think about its significance. Provide a template for the teacher to use in preparing a written report if the evaluation is being shared with others.

At some point in the process, the teacher may ask you why you don't just do the evaluation! This is another opportunity to explain that your job is to help others build capacity. In addition, share your belief that by doing the evaluation, the classroom teacher will have much more information about this student and about literacy. In addition, children are usually more comfortable in an evaluative setting with their own teacher. If the teacher is overwhelmed, offer to do a literacy-related activity with her class while she does part of the evaluation.

Occasionally, most literacy coaches will indeed do an evaluation of student literacies or will assist in doing parts of the evaluation. After all, we are all part of a larger school staff, and we all want to pitch in when needed. I encourage literacy coaches to be judicious in how often they do this; the goal should be to be helpful but not to do others' work for them or prevent others from learning more.

COVER SHEET FOR ASSESSMENT PACKET

[Note: This packet includes assessments for students PK–12; adjust as needed]

I have compiled the assessments in this folder as a resource for classroom teachers. Not all assessments will be useful to all teachers for all students. I'll be glad to help you decide which assessment tools to use.

Contents
Burke Reading Interview (Goodman, Watson, & Burke, 2005)
    Directions for Using the Burke Reading Interview
Reading Interest Survey (Rhodes, 1993)
Parent Survey/Interview (Rhodes, 1993)
Writing Interview (Rhodes, 1993)
Garfield Reading Attitude Survey (McKenna & Kear, 1999)
Miscue Summary Sheet (Wilde, 2000)
    Directions for Using the Miscue Summary Sheet
Miscue Analysis Sheet (Wilde, 2000)
    Directions for Using the Miscue Analysis Sheet
Retelling Directions (Goodman, Watson, & Burke, 2005)
Checklist of Observed Reading Behavior (Rhodes, 1993)
Suggestions for Evaluating Work Samples (Shea, Murray, & Harlin, 2005)
Reading Strategy Summary Sheet (Rhodes, 1993)
Think-Aloud Evaluation (Johnston, 1997)
Writing Process Observation Forms (Rhodes, 1993)
Analytic Writing Rubric (from state assessment)
Concepts of Print Evaluation (Clay, 2002)
Student Self-Evaluations (Davies, Cameron, Politano, & Gregory, 1992)

The Literacy Coach's Desk Reference: Processes and Perspectives for Effective Coaching by Cathy A. Toll
© 2006 National Council of Teachers of English.

Section 7: Conclusion

This brief concluding chapter provides key ideas to recall from the earlier sections of the book and closing statements from the author.

26 Conclusion

As I come to the end of writing this book, I am reflecting upon whether I have accomplished my goals. Of course, I can't really know this without feedback from readers. However, I'd like to summarize the concepts, beliefs, and practices related to literacy coaching that I've tried to emphasize in the previous pages.

- Literacy coaching is most effective when it begins with teachers' interests, needs, and concerns, and, therefore, literacy coaches are wise to develop the habit of listening and learning before all else.

- The goal of literacy coaching is to strengthen teachers' capacities by developing existing and new strengths.

- Good teaching is about problem finding and problem solving, and literacy coaches can help teachers refine both skills.

- Literacy coaches do much of their work in conversation with teachers, either individually or in groups.

- Literacy coaching conversations can be expanded through book study, extended inquiry, demonstration lessons, or co-teaching.

- The most effective demonstration lessons are those that build from coaching conversations and, therefore, support teachers in meeting goals that they have identified.

- Literacy coaches may be asked to perform duties for the entire school or for individual students, and they may choose to do those duties for a variety of reasons. However, when literacy coaches are not helping teachers—their true clients—they are not coaching. Wise coaches look for opportunities to connect non-coaching tasks with their true coaching work. In addition, these coaches monitor their work to ensure that an appropriate amount of time is indeed still available for their coaching duties.

If I have done my job well, readers of this book will understand my perspective on these points. More importantly, though, they will have practical strategies to make these ideas effective in their work.

Literacy coaching begins with relationships and trust. However, those elements are not enough. Literacy coaches also must have a repertoire of strategies to use in their work, and good coaches are wise to refine their craft over time by being reflective decision makers in their work.

The joy of literacy coaching is in collaborating with a variety of other professionals and in watching ourselves grow and change as a result. This is my joy in writing about literacy coaching as well. I would enjoy hearing your response to this book—both to share your growth and to understand how I might do my work better. Please feel free to write to me at toll@insightbb.com.

Happy coaching!

Appendix A: Managing Mandated Observation of Teachers

Some programs of literacy coaching mandate that coaches observe teachers in their classrooms. Such mandates are frequent in Reading First programs, for example. However, Showers and Joyce concluded from their work that, when two adults are in the classroom and only one of them is teaching, it should be the coach (1996). I find their observation to be useful. When literacy coaches are perceived as observers, they take on a role that parallels that of a supervisor as well as an expert and judge. Being perceived in these ways—or actually behaving in these manners—will limit literacy coaches' effectiveness. They will be distanced from teachers and struggle to have coaching conversations that are collaborative. Teachers may look to them for "the answers" but will not be likely to turn to such literacy coaches for support or mutual reflection or to discuss significant problems that trouble the teachers.

If you must observe in classrooms due to program mandates, I suggest one or more of the following:

- Take no notes; carry nothing if possible. This will reduce the impression that you are making supervisory observations.
- Watch the students more than the teacher.
- Explain in advance that you are required to observe and ask teachers how to make those classroom visits most helpful to them.
- Observe at times when the teacher is not providing whole-group instruction, which is the time when traditional supervisory observations often take place.
- Ask the teacher to suggest times that she or he would prefer you visit the classroom.
- Interact with students while in the classroom—perhaps by conferencing informally with one or two—to place your focus on aspects of the classroom other than the teacher.
- Ask the teacher if you can read a story to the class and consider the observations you make during that time to meet the requirement that you observe the classroom.

- Develop a voice with the leaders of your program and look for opportunities to engage them in rethinking the mandate that observations take place.

Appendix B: Separating Coaching from Supervising

work with literacy coaches all over the United States. These coaches are employed by their schools or districts to support teacher growth in literacy instruction. As a coach of literacy coaches, I can predict many of the questions that I will be asked because certain topics in coaching are common across sites. Among these common questions are a number that relate to coaching and supervision. Typical questions include:

- How can I convince teachers that I'm not working with them as a supervisor?
- How often should I report to the principal and how much should I tell her?
- What should I do if my principal wants me to tell him which teachers are not doing a good job?
- What should I do when I see something "bad" happening in a classroom? If I tell the principal, the teachers won't trust me.

At the core of such questions are two issues: (1) coaching duties sometimes look similar to duties performed by supervisors, and (2) coaches need to maintain teachers' trust while having good communication with the supervisor (Lyons & Pinnell, 2001; Toll, 2005). Let's explore these issues.

First, though, I'd like to provide my definitions of *coach* and *supervisor*. The definitions pertain specifically to work with teachers.

> **Coach:** One who helps teachers recognize what they know and can do, assists teachers as they strengthen their ability to make more effective use of what they know and do, and supports teachers as they learn more and do more.

> **Supervisor:** One who ensures that teachers meet the requirements of their positions at a satisfactory level and continue to do so over time.

I've given these definitions a good deal of thought. I have chosen to describe a coach in positive terms rather than terms that would indicate a

---

An earlier version of this appendix appeared as an article in *English Leadership Quarterly* 27(2). It is reprinted here by permission of the National Council of Teachers of English.

coach's duties in finding problems or helping underperforming teachers do better jobs. This choice reflects my belief that coaching builds on
strengths and that, while coaches may work with problem situations, they
don't necessarily do so. The definition above does not preclude working
with problem situations—they certainly can arise as a coach "assists
teachers in strengthening their ability to make more effective use of what
they know and do," as well as when a coach "supports teachers as they
learn more and do more."

I've phrased the definition of a supervisor in a similarly positive
manner. In addition, I've indicated that supervisors want to ensure that
teachers do their work satisfactorily not only in the present but also in
the future. The inclusion of "over time" in the definition indicates that
growth, not stasis, is a goal of supervision. I included another word, *satisfactory*, with a great deal of thought. Many teachers perform work that
is better than satisfactory, and many supervisors want above-satisfactory
work. I'd suggest, though, that when supervisors assist teachers in moving *beyond* satisfactory performance, they are really coaching, according
to the definitions above. In addition, when supervisors assist teachers in
continuing *satisfactory* performance over time, they may do some coaching as defined above, or they may continue to use supervisory strategies.

The examples below provide an illustration of the potential overlap between coaching and supervising in a principal's duties. The difference is subtle but important: When one is coaching, one is responding to another's needs, values, and perceptions. Yes, a coach will provide
her own perspective as well, but the teacher directs the content of the
conversation. In supervising, the supervisor may listen to and respect
another's needs, values, and perceptions, but the supervisor directs the
content of the conversation.

Drawing a Distinction between Supervising and Coaching

Example 1: Principal Supervising Only

Principal to third-year teacher: You have been really successful in getting your students interested in reading! Your classroom is full of interesting books, and the parents are involved, too. I know this was a
goal you've been working on—congratulations on your success. Now,
how do you plan to maintain the students' motivation to read?
[In this case, the principal follows an observation that the teacher met
his goal with a question to direct the teacher to a further goal.]

Example 2: Principal Supervising and Coaching

Principal to third-year teacher: You have been really successful in getting your students interested in reading! Your classroom is full of interesting books, and the parents are involved, too. What is your next goal for your literacy instruction?

[In this case, the principal follows an observation that the teacher met his goal with a question to get the teacher to think about what else he may want to address about his work.]

The reverse can also occur. A coach may slip into a supervisory role. Examples below exemplify the potential for such an overlap. In the first case, the coach responds to the teacher in a nonjudgmental manner and asks an inquiring question to help the teacher solve the problem. In the second case, the coach tells the teacher what to do.

Supervisors who act as coaches are rarely blundering, unless they are failing to perform their supervisory roles as well. However, coaches who slip into supervisory roles are usually making a mistake, often a serious mistake. Successful coaching depends upon trust between teachers and coaches (Costa & Garmston, 2002; Sweeney, 2003); if the teacher believes the coach is a supervisor, that trust may be jeopardized. In addition, when a coach becomes directive, the teacher may feel that his needs or concerns are not the focus of attention (Flaherty, 1998). Finally, coaching is new to the culture of many schools, and staff members often feel suspicious about claims that the coach is there to help. In such situations, when a coach behaves like a supervisor, even subtly, those suspicions flare, and the entire coaching endeavor is compromised.

For coaching to be successful, it must be separated from supervision. Coaches and supervisors can practice a number of strategies to make this possible. The remainder of this article provides such strategies.

Tips for Coaches

1. Separate yourself from the performance assessment of teachers. Do not participate in any aspect of others' performance assessment process.

2. If you see a supervisory matter, trust that the supervisor will see it, too. That's the supervisor's job—leave it up to her to take care of it. (Exceptions occur in cases where children are being endangered or where the coach needs to protect himself.)

3. Communicate with supervisors in a neutral manner.

- Provide a written summary of coaching meetings—individual and group—to those involved and to the principal routinely. Develop a one-page form that includes the names of participants, date of meeting, topics discussed, goals set, and action steps. Plans for the next meeting could also be included. *This information needs to be reported in a factual manner, emphasizing only positive steps taken and avoiding any statements of judgment.*

- Summarize coaching activities as a whole (or by grade level or department, if there are great differences in the work you do among such groups). This summary might include the number of individual coaching sessions, group coaching sessions, demonstration lessons, and other duties performed by a coach. Don't mention teachers' names. Give a copy to all staff members.

- Consider having a coach's advisory team with a broad range of representation that will help you evaluate the coaching *process* (*not* you or your colleagues) and report on the process to supervisors and staff.

4. In difficult situations with teachers, you can avoid acting like a supervisor while taking steps to move ahead by:

  - Asking a peer (teacher or coach) to sit in on a meeting and provide feedback as a critical friend. If you can, ask the teacher with whom you are working to agree to this and even to set it up.

  - Discussing with the teacher your concern and asking how to move beyond it. Focus on observable behaviors and your responses (*not* your guess about why the teacher is resisting, nor what you think the teacher is thinking/feeling).

  - Working with that teacher one-on-one rather than in a group, which will lessen the negative influence on others.

  - Inviting the teacher to take a leadership role in sharing successful practices or leading a study group (a risk—this could backfire).

  - Discussing the matter with the teacher's supervisor *if* you and the supervisor can be sure that the other will not in any way reveal to others that the conversation took place. (Do this rarely and only as a last resort.)

5. If a supervisor tells you that a teacher needs your help in improving performance to the satisfactory level, politely tell the supervisor that you'll wait for the teacher to approach you about the matter and then you'll be glad to help. (You may need to respectfully remind the supervisor about the need for a coach to avoid supervisory duties and point out that, if you approach the teacher, you will be acting as the representative of the supervisor.)

6. If a supervisor repeatedly asks you to perform activities that are supervisory in nature, ask for assistance in clarifying your role from the director of literacy or the director of coaching in your school district.

Demonstrating the Potential for Overlap between Supervising and Coaching

Example 3: Coach Coaching Only

Coach to ninth-grade English teacher: At this point in the school year, it may be helpful to look back at your students' cumulative writing folders to look at the samples you've collected.

Teacher: Oh! I forgot to collect samples all year!

Coach: Hmmm . . .

Teacher: I have had the students write like crazy, but because I'm new to this school, I forgot to put them in the cumulative folder.

Coach: What could you do now?

Example 4: Coach Coaching and Supervising

Coach to ninth-grade English teacher: At this point in the school year, it may be helpful to look back at your students' cumulative writing folders to look at the samples you've collected.

Teacher: Oh! I forgot to collect samples all year!

Coach: You're supposed to collect three of them. You need to see your department chair about this one.

Tips for Supervisors

1. If you believe that a teacher you are supervising needs to work with the literacy coach in order to improve performance to a satisfactory level:

   - Place responsibility in the hands of the teacher, not the coach, to initiate the coaching conversation. Avoid telling the coach that the teacher needs help and expecting the coach to approach the teacher. Ensure that the teacher knows the remediation effort is her responsibility and that the coach will be available to help.

   - Ask the teacher to outline who will do what in the improvement process.

   - Ask the teacher to provide notes of his work with the coach. (*Don't* ask the coach to do this).

2. Meet regularly with the coach and be aware of coaching activities in general. Learn about the nature of the coach's work, including areas of success and struggle, without asking about specific supervisory problems.

3. If the coach broaches the topic of a particular teacher, ask whether the teacher should be the one sharing the information with the supervisor.

4. Don't require the coach to "report" on individual teachers.

5. Don't share confidential supervisory information with the coach.

References

Costa, A., & Garmston, R. (2002). *Cognitive coaching: A foundation for renaissance schools* (2nd ed.). Norwood, MA: Christopher-Gordon.

Flaherty, J. (1998). *Coaching: Evoking excellence in others.* Boston: Butterworth-Heinemann.

Lyons, C. A., & Pinnell, G. S. (2001). *Systems for change in literacy education: A guide to professional development.* Portsmouth, NH: Heinemann.

Sweeney, D. (2003). *Learning along the way: Professional development by and for teachers.* Portland, ME: Stenhouse.

Toll, C. A. (2005). *The literacy coach's survival guide: Essential questions and practical answers.* Newark, DE: International Reading Association.

Note

This article was originally published in *Leadership Quarterly, 27*, 2 (October 2004), pages 5–7.

Appendix C: Annotated Bibliography

I offer here a selection of materials that I find particularly helpful for literacy coaching.

Books

Achinstein, B. (2002). *Community diversity and conflict among schoolteachers: The ties that blind*. New York: Teachers College Press.

Examines the complexity of collaboration and theorizes why collaborative work is difficult.

Boreen, J., Johnson, M. K., Niday, D., & Potts, J. (2000). *Mentoring beginning teachers: Guiding, reflecting, coaching*. Portland, ME: Stenhouse.

Although focused on mentoring, which is similar to but not the same as coaching, this book provides some useful strategies for encouraging reflection and mirroring.

Carter, J. (2003). *Nasty people: How to stop being hurt by them without becoming one of them*. New York: McGraw-Hill.

A quirky book that makes one think about how difficult situations arise between people—and how to stop them.

Ellsworth, E. (1997). *Teaching positions: Difference, pedagogy, and the power of address*. New York: Teachers College Press.

Read this book if you have read the familiar materials on collaboration and want to think in deeper, more complex, and theoretical ways about what makes collaboration, particularly communicative dialogue, so difficult.

Flaherty, J. (1999). *Coaching: Evoking excellence in others*. Boston: Butterworth-Heinemann.

Although written for coaches in all fields, this book provides some excellent insights and resources for literacy coaches, including thoughts about resistance, respect, and listening, a great reading list, and a coach's self-assessment.

Foucault, M. (1980). *Power/knowledge: Selected interviews and other writings, 1972–1977*. New York: Pantheon.

> Readers who want to think more deeply about power will find the chapter on truth and power provocative.

Hargreaves, A. (1994). *Changing teachers, changing times: Teachers' work and culture in the postmodern age*. New York: Teachers College Press.

> I return to this book often to review Hargreaves description of the tensions that occur when school staffs try to alter their ways of working together and alone.

Larner, M. (2004). *Pathways: Charting a course for professional learning*. Portsmouth, NH: Heinemann.

> Coaches will find this book to be a handy addition to their professional library when they want to think about the overall professional development program.

Rodgers, E. M., & Pinnell, G. S. (Eds.). (2002). *Learning from teaching in literacy education: New perspectives on professional development*. Portsmouth, NH: Heinemann.

> Like the book by Larner, this book provides big-picture perspective on professional development and a chapter about literacy coaching using models different from the ones in my work.

Stone, D., Patton, B., & Heen, S. (1999). *Difficult conversations: How to discuss what matters most*. New York: Penguin.

> This book provides background on communicating in organizations and with individuals that might help literacy coaches refine some of their practices.

Sweeney, D. (2003). *Learning along the way: Professional development by and for teachers*. Portland, ME: Stenhouse.

> Sweeney tells of her literacy coaching experiences while describing her model for gradual release of responsibility.

Toll, C. A. (2005). *The literacy coach's survival guide: Essential questions and practical answers*. Newark, DE: International Reading Association.

> My first book on literacy coaching, it provides a perspective on coaching and working with a variety of teachers, as well as thinking about the change process.

Wheatley, M. J., & Kellner-Rogers, M. (1996). *A simpler way*. San Francisco: Berrett-Koehler.

> The authors present systems theory in a manner that makes one believe such thinking could truly transform society, including schools.

Internet Resources

Edna McConnell Clark Foundation, www.emcf.org.

> Reports studies on programs to support low-income youth, including one report on literacy coaching: *Making our own road: The emergence of school-based staff developers in America's public schools* at http://www.emcf.org/pdf/student_ourownroadbw.pdf.

International Reading Association: www.reading.org.

> IRA's position statement on reading specialists addresses literacy coaches; standards for middle school and high school literacy coaches can also be found at this site.

National Council of Teachers of English: www.ncte.org.

> This site includes many articles and resources on literacy coaching as well as other topics of importance to literacy coaches. Click on "Literacy Coaching" on the list of Teaching Resource Collections.

National Staff Development Council: www.nsdc.org.

> A great deal of information on a variety of professional development topics. Terry Greene's literature review on coaching can be found by entering "literacy coaching" in the search window.

Toll and Associates: www.tollandassociates.com.

> Please visit my Web site to access newsletters, learn about workshops, and read about my work.

References

Achinstein, B. (2002). *Community diversity and conflict among schoolteachers: The ties that blind*. New York: Teachers College Press.

Allen, J. (2004). *Tools for teaching content literacy*. Portland, ME: Stenhouse.

Barrett, M. (1991). *The politics of truth: From Marx to Foucault*. Stanford, CA: Stanford University Press.

Beck, I. L., McKeown, M. G., and Kucan, L. (2002). *Bringing words to life: Robust vocabulary instruction*. New York: Guilford.

Birchak, B., Connor, C., Crawford, K. M., Kahn, L., Kaiser, S., Turner, S., & Short, K. (1998). *Teacher study groups: Building community through dialogue and reflection*. Urbana, IL: National Council of Teachers of English.

Bracey, G. W. (2004). *Setting the record straight: Responses to misconceptions about public education in the United States* (2nd ed.). Portsmouth, NH: Heinemann.

Carelli, A. O. (2004). *The truth about supervision: Coaching, teamwork, interviewing, appraisals, 360 degree assessments, and recognition*. Springfield, IL: Charles C. Thomas.

Carnoy, M. (1974). *Education as cultural imperialism*. New York: David McKay.

Central Regional Reading First Technical Assistance Center. (2005). *Leading for reading success: An introductory guide for Reading First coaches*. Portsmouth, NH: RMC Corporation.

Chandler, K., & the Mapleton Teacher-Research Group. (1999). *Spelling inquiry: How one elementary school caught the mnemonic plague*. Portland, ME: Stenhouse.

Clay, M. M. (2002). *An observation survey of early literacy achievement*. Portsmouth, NH: Heinemann.

Clift R. T., Houston, W. R., & Pugach, M. C. (Eds.). (1990). *Encouraging reflective practice in education: An analysis of issues and programs*. New York: Teachers College Press.

Cochran-Smith, M., & Lytle, S. L. (1993). *Inside/outside: Teacher research and knowledge*. New York: Teachers College Press.

Cunningham, P. M., & Hall, D. P. (2005). *Making words: Lessons for home or school (grade 3)*. Greesboro, NC: Carson-Dellosa.

Davies, A., Cameron, C., Politano, C., & Gregory, K. (1992). *Together is better: Collaborative assessment, evaluation, and reporting*. Winnipeg, Manitoba: Portage and Main.

De Dreu, C. K. W., & De Vries, N. K. (1997). Minority dissent in organizations. In C. K. W. De Dreu & E. Van De Vliert (Eds.), *Using conflict in organizations*. Thousand Oaks, CA: Sage.

DiPardo, A. (1997). Of war, doom, and laughter: Images of collaboration in the public-school workplace. *Teacher Education Quarterly, 24,* 89–104.

Foucault, M. (1980). *Power/knowledge: Selected interviews and other writings, 1972–1977.* New York: Pantheon.

Fridjhon, M., & Fuller, F. (2004). The geography of relationships: A primer for coaching the true nature of relationship diversity. Presented at the International Coaching Federation, Quebec City, Quebec. http://www.coachfederation.org/2004proceedings/icf_data/pages/trackc/FridjhonFullerhandout.pdf (retrieved June 9, 2005).

Garmston, R. J. (2005). *The presenter's fieldbook: A practical guide* (2nd ed.). Norwood, MA: Christopher-Gordon.

Garvin, D. A., & Roberto, M. A. (2005). Change through persuasion. *Harvard Business Review, 83*(2), 104–112.

Gee, J. P. (1999). *Social linguistics and literacies: Ideology in discourses* (2nd ed.). London: Falmer.

Goodman Y. M., Watson, D. J., & Burke, C. L. (2005). *Reading miscue inventory: From evaluation to instruction.* Katonah, NY: Richard C. Owen.

Hord, S. M., Rutherford, W. L., Huling-Austin, L., & Hall, G. E. (1987). *Taking charge of change.* Alexandria, VA: Association for Supervision and Curriculum Development.

Hubbard, R. S., & Power, B. M. (2003). *The art of classroom inquiry: A handbook for teacher researchers* (Rev. ed.). Portsmouth, NH: Heinemann.

Indiana Department of Education. (n.d.). *Strategic and continuous school improvement and achievement plan,* Indianapolis, IN, http://www.doe.state.in.us/asap/sip2.html#Required (retrieved June 1, 2005).

Johnston, P. H. (1997). *Knowing literacy: Constructive literacy assessment.* Portland, ME: Stenhouse.

Joyce, B., & Showers, B. (2002). *Student achievement through staff development* (3rd ed.). Alexandria, VA: Association for Supervision and Curriculum Development.

Learning First Alliance. (2000). *Every child reading: A professional development guide.* Washington, DC: Author.

Leonard, N. H., Beauvais, L. L., & Scholl, R. W. (1995). A self concept-based model of work motivation. Paper presented at the Annual Meeting of the Academy of Management, Vancouver, BC. http://www.cba.uri.edu/Scholl/Papers/Self_Concept_Motivation.HTM (retrieved April 29, 2005).

Loucks-Horsley, S., Love, N., Stiles, K. E., Mundry, S., & Hewson, P. W. (2003). *Designing professional development for teachers of science and mathematics* (2nd ed.). Thousand Oaks, CA: Corwin.

Luke, A. (1995). When basic skills and information processing just aren't enough: Rethinking reading in new times. *Teachers College Record, 97,* 95–115.

Lyons, C. A., & Pinnell, G. S. (2001). *Systems for change in literacy education: A guide to professional development.* Portsmouth, NH: Heinemann.

McKenna, M. C., & Kear, D. J. (1999). Measuring attitude toward reading: A new tool for teachers. In S. J. Barrentine, Ed., *Reading assessment: Principles and practices for elementary teachers.* Newark, DE: International Reading Association.

National Center on Education and the Economy. (2002). *Comprehensive reform designs.* Washington, DC: Author.

National Commission on Excellence in Education (1983). *A nation at risk: The imperatives of educational reform.* Washington, DC: U.S. Department of Education.

National Staff Development Council. (2001). *NSDC's standards for staff development* (Rev. ed.). Oxford, OH: Author.

North Central Regional Educational Laboratory. (2004). *Reading coaches and professional development,* http://www.ncrel.org/rf/pd/training.htm (retrieved May 12, 2005).

Palmer, P. (1993). *To know as we are known: Education as a spiritual journey.* San Francisco: HarperCollins.

Rhodes, L. K. (1993). *Literacy Assessment: A handbook of instruments.* Portsmouth, NH: Heinemann.

Shannon, P. (1998). *Reading poverty.* Portsmouth, NH: Heinemann.

Shea, M., Murray, R., & Harlin, R. (2005). *Drowning in data: How to collect, organize, and document student performance.* Portsmouth, NH: Heinemann.

Short, K. G., & Harste, J. C., with Burke, C. (1996). *Creating classrooms for authors and inquirers* (2nd ed.). Portsmouth, NH: Heinemann.

Showers, B., & Joyce, B. (1996). The evolution of peer coaching. *Educational Leadership, 53*(6), 12–16.

Sircus, M. A. (2005) *Mirroring and the art of listening,* at http://www.worldpsychology.net/World%20Psychology/VirtualPsyFiles/ayahuasc22.htm (retrieved May 8, 2005).

Sparks, D., & Loucks-Horsley, S. (1990). Models of staff development. In R. Houston (Ed.), *Handbook of research on teacher education* (3rd ed., pp. 234–250). New York: Macmillan.

Spring, J. (1997). *Political agendas for education: From the Christian Coalition to the Green Party.* Mahwah, NH: Lawrence Erlbaum.

State of Washington Superintendent of Public Instruction. (n.d.). *School improvement,* Olympia, WA, http://www.k12.wa.us/SchoolImprovement/process.aspx (retrieved June 1, 2005).

Supovitz, J. A. (2002). Developing communities of instructional practice. *Teachers College Record, 104*, 1591–1626.

Sweeney, D. (2003). *Learning along the way: Professional development by and for teachers*. Portland, ME: Stenhouse.

Taberski, S. (2000). *On solid ground: Strategies for teaching reading K–3*. Portsmouth, NH: Heinemann.

Toll, C. A. (2005). *The literacy coach's survival guide: Essential questions and practical answers*. Newark, DE: International Reading Association.

Wilde, S. (2000). *Miscue analysis made easy: Building on student strengths*. Portsmouth, NH: Heinemann.

Zeichner, K. M., & Liston, D. P. (1996). *Reflective teaching: An introduction (Reflective teaching and the social conditions of schooling)*. Mahwah, NH: Lawrence Erlbaum.

Author

Cathy A. Toll is the founder and lead consultant of Toll and Associates, a firm committed to serving the needs of literacy coaches and those who support them. Prior to her leadership of Toll and Associates, she worked as a teacher at the elementary, middle, high school, and university levels; a reading specialist; a curriculum coordinator; a principal; director of literacy research and development; grant director; and consultant. This work provided many opportunities to deepen her understanding of literacy, learning, teaching, schools, and leadership and to refine her skills as an educational coach. Toll has a PhD from The Pennsylvania State University and engages in scholarly work related to teacher professional growth, educational change, and the politics of schools. Originally from Wisconsin, Toll makes her home in Normal, Illinois, where she bicycles whenever she can. At the time this book went to press, she had accepted the position of chair of teacher education at Indiana University–Purdue University Indianapolis.

This book was typeset in Palatino and Helvetica by Electronic Imaging.
Typefaces used on the cover were Bank Gothic and AGaramond Semibold.
The book was printed on 50-lb. Williamsburg Offset paper by Versa Press, Inc.